WEAPON

KATANA: THE SAMURAI SWORD

STEPHEN TURNBULL

Series Editor Martin Pegler

First published in Great Britain in 2010 by Osprey Publishing,
PO Box 883, Oxford, OX1 9PL, UK
PO Box 3985, New York, NY 10185-3985, USA
Email: info@ospreypublishing.com

Osprey Publishing, part of Bloomsbury Publishing Plc.

Transferred to digital print on demand 2014.

First published 2010
3rd impression 2014

Printed and bound by
Cadmus Communications, USA.

A CIP catalogue record for this book is available from the
British Library.

ISBN: 978 1 84908 151 1

Page layout by Ben Salvesen
Artwork by Johnny Shumate
Index by Alison Worthington
Originated by PDQ Media
Typeset in Sabon and Univers

The Woodland Trust
Osprey Publishing is supporting the Woodland Trust,
the UK's leading woodland conservation charity, by funding
the dedication of trees.

www.ospreypublishing.com

Dedication
To Hilary Taylor.

Acknowledgments
I have learned much about Japanese swords over the years
through my membership of the Token Society of Great Britain,
to whose officers and members I give thanks. With regard to my
more recent research, I wish to acknowledge in particular
the advice and support provided by the Royal Armouries
Museum, Leeds, and Osafune Sword Village in Okayama
Prefecture, Japan, where the traditions of the katana, from its
forging to its appreciation and assessment, are devotedly
maintained.

Cover illustration © Stephen Turnbull.
Katana photograph (top) © Royal Armouries.

All images in this book are from the author's collection.

CONTENTS

INTRODUCTION

The Japanese word 'katana' is that used most commonly to identify the deadly curved sword of the samurai: the final evolutionary stage of what is probably the finest edged weapon in world military history. The origins of the katana lay in the straight-bladed swords of ancient Japan, and from these straight swords the *tachi* evolved, which was the first type of Japanese sword to have a curved blade. *Tachi* would be slung from the belts of the early samurai – the members of Japan's knightly class. However, the transformation of the *tachi* into the katana had less to do with shape and construction than with mode of use. Changes in swordsmanship meant that the sword, sometimes in a shortened form, would be thrust into the belt with its cutting edge uppermost, rather than suspended from the belt. Now the samurai could deliver a deadly swordstroke as part of the action of drawing his weapon, rather than having to execute a two-handed movement of unsheathing and preparation. Such was the weapon that was to become the sword of legend.

Not surprisingly, the legends and traditions surrounding the katana are inseparable from the culture of the men who wore and used it, because no edged weapon in history has been more closely associated with its owner than the Japanese sword has been with the samurai. To a samurai, one's katana was both a weapon and a symbol. Never has the relationship between man and sword been better expressed than in the words of the great *shogun* (military dictator) of Japan, Tokugawa Ieyasu (1542–1616), who advised his successors that 'the sword is the soul of the warrior'. No samurai would ever be without his sword, whether he was wearing armour or everyday clothes, and a sword forged by a celebrated master was one of the most precious gifts a warrior could receive. The sword, in its rest position thrust into the belt, would tell the world that its owner was a true samurai – a member of a social and military elite – since members of the lower classes did not carry weapons (theoretically, at least).

When the katana was drawn from the scabbard – an event that actually occurred mercifully less often than the movies would have us believe – it became the ultimate means of asserting the samurai's authority.

The katana was also one of the few edged weapons in history that could be used both as a sword and as a shield: the blade's resilient and springy inner core meant that the weapon could absorb considerable shock. This factor would not have been present had the entire blade possessed the extreme hardness of the sword's very sharp cutting edge. In a combat situation the samurai's first stroke, delivered straight from the scabbard, could be employed either to parry an opponent's strike or to provide its owner's own devastating first and final blow – one that would likely save his own life and end that of another.

The samurai was essentially an individual warrior, and the surviving great swords of Japan similarly have their own individuality: their shapes and polished surfaces with unique temper patterns provide a 'personality' as unique as the signatures of their makers on the tang.

The visual beauty of a sword, the outward expression of an inner power, was fully appreciated by interested European visitors to Japan in the latter half of the nineteenth century. Japan had closed its doors to the Western world for two centuries. Among the pioneers who visited the newly reopened country were enthusiasts for the Japanese martial arts, and swords provided the ultimate level of fascination. One admirer wrote in 1905 that 'as a weapon of offence and defence a katana is an infinitely superior one to the ridiculous, single-handed sword with its 36-inch blade, with which British infantry officers are armed'.

By 1905, of course, the katana had become more a symbol of military rank for the Japanese armed forces than an actual offensive weapon. Even in this much reduced role, the long tradition that equated a superlative weapon with a superlative warrior was continued. Paradoxically, however, even though the sword may have played a key symbolic role in the life of the samurai over many centuries, on most occasions when a samurai engaged in actual combat the sword was not the primary weapon of choice. The first samurai made up the private armies of the rich landowners from the ninth century onwards, and they came to cherish and respect most of all the prowess a warrior displayed in *kyuba no michi* ('the way of bow and horse'). The ability to deliver arrows from horseback was the military skill that would win most battles, and it was only when the bow, with no arrows left, was passed to an attendant that the samurai would draw his two-handed sword and engage in combat with edged weapons. It is not until the attempted invasions of Japan by the Mongol armies of Khubilai Khan during the thirteenth century that we read of swords being chosen as the primary weapon, and this only when the samurai engaged the Mongols in hand-to-hand fighting on the decks of their ships. Yet for every recorded heroic swordfight with a Mongol warrior, there is an equivalent story of a different samurai felling an invader from a distance using a well-delivered arrow.

Three centuries later, during Japan's sixteenth-century Sengoku Period – the 'Age of Warring States' – the outcome of battles depended on the

This hanging scroll from Shimada Art Museum, Kumamoto, shows Miyamoto Musashi, the most famous and enigmatic of the *kengo*, in characteristic pose armed with a sword in each hand. Musashi was renowned for his ability to wield a katana and a *wakizashi* at the same time.

deployment of large infantry squads armed with firearms, bows or long spears, and units of mounted samurai who wielded spears from the saddle in preference to bows. Once again the sword was the secondary battlefield weapon. The primary weapon was now the straight-bladed spear, and it is really only in actions undertaken off the battlefield – such as revenge killings or duels – that we encounter the popular image of the individual samurai warrior squarely facing his opponent with sword in hand. Nevertheless, despite the practicalities of the battlefield, the ideal of the samurai as a sword- rather than a spear- or even gun-wielding warrior was to be cherished long after the introduction of modern weapons had made the sword an anachronism. Thus, the battle of Kariwano – the final conflict of the Boshin War of 1868 – finished with a suicidal charge using swords, and during the Satsuma Rebellion of 1877 the followers of Saigo Takamori climbed the walls of Kumamoto Castle, katana in hand, to receive the bullets of the imperial army.

DEVELOPMENT

Katana: the soul of the samurai

Even for the uninitiated, the first encounter with a fine katana cannot fail to provoke the kind of impressions that the Japanese sword has inspired throughout history. A single glance will suffice to convince the newcomer that here is an object that, with its icy sheen and inner strength, is both a weapon and a work of art. Add to this two further realizations – that the artistry that created its complex surface appearance directly reflects the quest for perfection in a weapon, and that the techniques that first brought all this about are today lost to history and merely presumed – and one's appreciation of the object's uniqueness is complete.

The metallurgy underlying a Japanese sword is exceedingly complex and finds visual expression in the surface anatomy of the final blade. Every detail of the finish has some bearing on the sword's quality, and the development of these microtechniques has left a trail that can be traced back many centuries. Because of these qualities and the historical dimension they represent, this section of the book will start with the forging of a blade, thereby introducing the technical language that is required before one can fully appreciate the historical development of the sword from the straight-bladed weapon of antiquity to the curved blade of the katana.

THE MAKING OF A JAPANESE SWORD

Even though none of the actual techniques used by the early swordsmiths was apparently ever written down, the smiths' traditions are so strong that even today some superb swords are made using the presumed methodology of a past age. The creation of a fine katana was, and still is, a matter of tradition and religious solemnity. The presence within the swordmaker's

The premises of a sword polisher, whose craftsmen are putting the final touches to a fine blade using traditional techniques. The figure on the left is polishing a finished blade with a cloth, while the figure on the right is sharpening a blade using a whetstone and abrasive slurry. This is a print from the Meiji Period, based on a medieval painting.

forge of a *kamidana*, the Shinto 'god-shelf' found in many Japanese homes, proclaims that this is a sacred space; this is also acknowledged by the humility of the craftsman himself. As often as not he will refer to himself simply as a *kajiya* (blacksmith) rather than a *tosho* (swordsmith). The *kami* (deities) will first be invoked before the swordsmith, clad in white robes resembling those of a Shinto priest, begins the long and arduous process of transforming raw materials into one of the country's finest finished products.

Nowadays, steel for swords can be obtained from sources outside Japan. However, the early swordsmiths were also iron producers: the raw material for a Japanese sword came from the surrounding environment. Beside some rivers in the coastal areas, particularly along the edge of the Inland Sea, were to be found deposits of *satetsu* (iron sand). The term itself indicates the composition of the sand. This rare ore would be smelted in small primitive furnaces at 1300–1500°C to produce *tama hagane* (raw steel pieces). The best pieces, with a carbon content of 0.3–1.5 per cent, were then beaten into thin cakes, and the expert *tosho* would select the ones most suitable for swordmaking.

In this beautifully observed model in Aya Castle, Miyazaki Prefecture, we see a swordsmith kneeling while his assistant wields a large hammer. They are both dressed in ceremonial white robes and wear lacquered *eboshi* caps. The sacred atmosphere is confirmed by the *kamidana* (god shelf) on the wall behind them and the hanging *shimenawa* (sacred rope) that indicates that the space within the forge is holy ground.

Chemically speaking, steel is a combination of iron and carbon. Pure iron is too soft to be given a sharp edge. The more carbon is present, the harder the steel will be; however, too much carbon will make the sword brittle. The skill of the early Japanese swordsmiths lay in their ability to control the carbon content despite having no knowledge of modern metallurgical processes or access to microscopic viewing techniques. Quite how they achieved this will remain a mystery. However, the results of their work, in the form of the peerless weapons they made, provide amazing evidence of how successful they were. Another difference from modern steel-production methods is that the steel of a Japanese sword was never heated sufficiently highly to melt it, so in the finished product a degree of heterogeneity survived. Yet it was this very lack of uniformity that was to yield the classic weapons.

We now know that when steel with a carbon content of 0.7 per cent (the usual proportion found in Japanese swords) is heated to 750°C it becomes a substance known as austenite. This has an open crystalline structure and in it carbon atoms combine readily with iron. When austenite is cooled rapidly its crystalline structure changes so that it becomes

FAR LEFT
Tama hagane (raw steel pieces) resembling small flakes and produced from the smelting of *satetsu* (iron sand) are piled up ready to be put into the furnace so they will fuse together. (Osafune Sword Village)

LEFT
This demonstration piece shows how the repeated folding of the steel billet was achieved. The existing billet is notched using an axe above a frame and then beaten back on itself. (Osafune Sword Village)

One of the most dramatic demonstrations of the strength and resilience of the katana blade, a quality most cherished by the swordsmiths, was provided in 1860 when Ii Naosuke was assassinated by loyalist *ronin* as a punishment for his co-operation with Western powers. The attack took place just outside Edo Castle.

martensite – a compound that allows the locking of carbon molecules into the iron to produce the hardest form of steel. However, if austenite is allowed to cool slowly it produces, among other substances, a softer steel called pearlite. It was by producing these two forms of steel and then combining them to make a blade that the Japanese *tosho* were able to create a weapon with a super-hard cutting edge but also a resilient body that would absorb the shock of impact. The change in surface appearance along the length of a Japanese blade, a feature readily noticed when one examines a good specimen, marks the transitional zone between the martensite crystals of the hardened cutting edge and the softer pearlite of the body.

The basic structure of a Japanese sword is therefore a duplex one, with different types of steel, although multiple combinations are also to be found. The simplest twofold design has a soft inner core, the *shingane*, which has a lower carbon content than the outer skin, or *hadagane*. This outer surface is of harder steel that will provide a cutting edge; the softer inner core will give resilience.

Several of the finer points of a finished blade are illustrated by this fine example of a katana on display in the Kaisendo, Kaminoyama City, Yamagata Prefecture. There is a very pronounced temper pattern (*hamon*) that marks the interface between the harder steel of the cutting edge and the softer and more resilient steel of the body. The *shinogi* (ridge) runs along the blade to the *kissaki* (point).

The sections were created and initially treated similarly. First, the pieces of *tama hagane*, which look like rice crackers, were carefully piled up on a long spoon-like object with paper tied round them to hold them together until they were placed in the furnace. At a temperature of about 1300°C the pieces began to fuse together. The result of this was a basic block of steel. This was broken up and, after checking that any visible impurities had been removed, it was re-forged. The steel billet resulting from this was repeatedly heated and beaten. The billet was continuously folded back upon itself so as to create a complex structure with several layers. The folding was achieved by notching the red-hot billet using an axe-like implement and then hammering the billet against the angle.

The difference between the *hadagane* and the *shingane* in terms of processing lay simply in the number of foldings. The outer *hadagane* received the most foldings, which determined its relatively higher carbon content and its ultimate level of hardness.

Next, the two separate pieces were combined. This was sometimes done just by creating a U-shape within the *hadagane* into which the *shingane* would be inserted, or the outer skin might be wrapped around the inner. In swords of more complex design, other grades of steel were combined with the two skins to provide the sides and the back of the blade. Whatever method was used, the *hadagane* would enclose the core of the sword along its length until just short of the tip. The steel 'sandwich' was now heated and hammered again. The purpose of this was partly to ensure that no dirt or air pockets are caught between the two surfaces, but mainly to stretch the billet into its final elongated shape. Using immense skill born of long experience, the combined steels were slowly drawn out into the rough but recognizable outline of a Japanese blade. At this stage the shape was still rectangular – no curve had yet been added. A decisive step was the creation of the point (*kissaki*) by cutting off the end of the billet, leaving a triangular shape. This long proto-sword was called a *sunobe*.

A modern ink painting showing the forging of a sword at Osafune Sword Village, Okayama Prefecture.

Blow by blow, the defined, familiar shape of the classic samurai sword was slowly forced out of the *sunobe* as each of the components along its length was shaped. The sword back (*mune*) was made thicker than the cutting edge (*ha*). The interface between the smooth blade and the rougher tang that would eventually lie concealed within the handle also soon became evident. Most importantly, the curve was now starting to become evident all along the length of the blade. This process had to be strictly controlled so that the sword took the shape the smith desired: it must not be too pronounced or too shallow. The work then changed from heavy beating to filing and scraping, to produce – among other features – the *shinogi* (central ridge). Eventually the crude blade was now in a clearly recognizable form.

Now is the moment when the sword essentially springs into life: when the selective hardening of the cutting edge takes place. No other stage in the katana's

In this fascinating detail from an illustration in a woodblock version of *Hojo Godaiki* we see samurai of the Hojo family sharpening the blades of their swords before going into battle. They are using whetstones similar to those that would have been employed by the swords' makers to give the blades their first polishing and sharpening.

creation was so shrouded in mystery, or as dependent upon the *tosho*'s experience. Any steel blade can be hardened by heating it to the desired temperature and then plunging it into cold water, but to prevent the entire blade experiencing the high rate of cooling sought for the cutting edge only, a straightforward yet very precise operation was carried out. The entire blade was carefully coated in slurry clay. Then clay is removed just from the edge area that was to be hardened, in such a way that wave patterns will appear in the interface between the body of the sword and its edge. The precise thickness of differential clay layer to be used, the exact immersion period, the crucial temperature of the steel (said to be about 730°C) and the temperature of the water into which the steel would be thrust were all a matter of lore and experience, and together served almost as a swordmaker's signature. Assessing the blade's temperature was done purely by eye, so at this stage the forge was deliberately plunged into darkness. As for the equally vital matter of water temperature, one of the many legends about the old swordsmiths tells of the greedy apprentice who tried to discover the secret of the correct temperature of the trough by putting his fingers into it, and was instantly punished by having his hand cut off by a sword stroke from the furious master.

One of the most noticeable features of the surface of a fine blade is the presence of apparent irregularities in the finish. The untrained observer might surmise that these are flaws; however, they are actually a key visual aspect of the sword, resulting from the above manufacturing process, that confirms the weapon's quality. The process of tempering means that the boundary between the two degrees of hardness is revealed in the edge pattern, called the *hamon*; in the zone where the temper pattern and the steel surface meet, *nie* and *nioi* appear. *Nie* are relatively coarse granular particles visible to the naked eye; *nioi* are microscopic particles. *Nie* have been compared poetically to individual stars shining in the sky, while the presence of *nioi* is indicated by a misty line like the Milky Way. The various formations made by these grains are a matter to which a traditional swordsmith would devote a great deal of effort, and add greatly to a sword's aesthetic appeal.

The blade was now ready to receive its polished finish and its edge. The first stage of polishing, the removal of scale and metal, was done by rubbing on a very coarse abrasive stone. At this point the blade's curvature could be adjusted by heating the back and pressing the blade against a copper block. If desired, grooves might be cut into the blade surface. Polishing and sharpening continued using a succession of finer-grained stones until the stage of final polishing was undertaken. Over this, much secrecy was maintained. Then, the selectively hardened cutting area could finally be whetted to produce a degree of sharpness without parallel anywhere in the world. With the maker's work complete, the tang would normally have inscribed upon it his signature and the date of manufacture or some other comment. However, the presence of a famous name on a blade does not automatically identify the swordsmith. There may have been attempts at deception through forged signatures, but there was also the factor of the tremendous respect accorded to a master by his pupils. This could mean that even when a hugely talented student who had surpassed his teacher became a swordsmith in his own right, he might still inscribe a prized blade with his master's name out of respect and gratitude.

The finished blade was mounted in a *tsuka* (handle) to produce the weapon that is so familiar today. A *tsuba* (sword guard) protected the hands, while cord twisted around the handle over a layer of *same* (the skin of the giant ray) provided a secure grip for the user. A made-to-measure scabbard (*saya*) was created out of magnolia wood. Testing of swords would be carried out to ensure that they had the correct balance and would cut effectively. In ancient times the cutting test could be carried out on live bodies – those of condemned criminals – but it was far more common to have the sword's power tested on corpses, or on bundles of rushes bound around a bamboo core.

EARLY SWORDS AND THE DEVELOPMENT OF THE *TACHI* STYLE

The techniques described above, used in making a katana today, are believed to be very similar to the methods used by the ancient swordsmiths. This is impossible to confirm because the secrets of swordmaking were passed on orally from a master to his chosen pupil, and this continuity was broken with the end of the time of civil wars, at the beginning of the seventeenth century. Also, few swords from the earlier age have survived, and it would be unthinkable to subject them to destructive analysis.

TOP
A *horimono* (carved decoration) appears next to the tang on this fine example of a *tachi* blade. The design features a dragon curled around a spear.

MIDDLE
Adding the swordmaker's signature to the rough area of the tang that would be enclosed within the handle was the final process carried out on a blade by the swordsmith himself.

BOTTOM
The early *tachi*-style swords were traditionally fitted with ornate sword furniture, as shown on this modern example. The scabbard and hilt are lacquered and gilded.

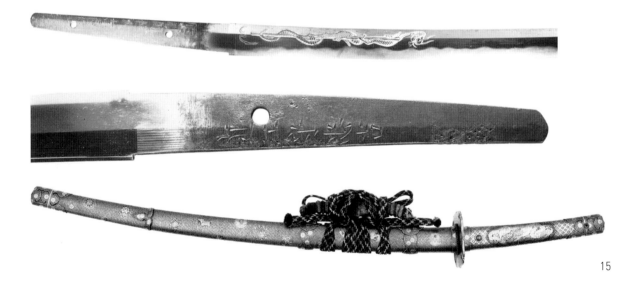

15

However, the specimens that have survived do let us trace the katana's evolution over almost two millennia. One of the most precious ancient metal objects to be preserved in Japan is a sword. It is owned by the Isonokami Shrine in Tenri, Nara Prefecture, and bears a date equivalent to AD 369. Clearly a ceremonial weapon rather than a sword made for fighting, it has a blade with seven branches and is believed to be a gift from the King of Baekje, one of the 'Three Kingdoms' that then shared the Korean peninsula. Japanese tradition associates it with Empress Jingu, the warrior empress who is supposed to have led a military expedition to Korea. The semi-legendary figure of Jingu, who may represent an authentic type of female shamanistic ruler, is also associated with a war fought to ensure the succession of her son, Emperor Ojin. In the campaign against his rivals she fooled the enemy into discarding their swords after Jingu's army had apparently abandoned theirs as a gesture of goodwill. However, these swords were only wooden replicas, and her army then took up their real swords and gained the victory.

Swords with seven branches or wooden blades are a far cry from the fighting weapons that undoubtedly did exist in the early days. The *Wei Zhi* (the chronicle of the Wei dynasty of China) mentions swords in certain passages dealing with the country of Wa, as Japan was then known. As early as AD 239 we read of Queen Himiko (or Pimiko), Japan's female ruler at the time, accepting gifts from the Wei of a gold seal, silk, mirrors and swords. Not long after this we find the beginnings of the Japanese tradition of burying deceased rulers in large tombs (*kofun*) that resembled artificial mountains. Excavation of *kofun* has yielded several swords. As is implied by the record of a gift from the Wei, these swords are Chinese in style and are likely to be of Chinese manufacture, a contention supported by inscriptions on some of them. The *kofun*-era swords have been given the name *chokuto* by modern scholars. These weapons are straight-bladed and 70–80cm long, with a triangular cross-section and only one of their two edges sharpened. The widest difference between types appears in pommel design. Some have a characteristic ring-shaped pommel, while others are made with variously shaped tangs that fit into separate hilts. These swords are totally unlike the later classic Japanese weapon, with its characteristic curved shape.

China's greatest gift to Japan was the Buddhist religion and the richness of culture associated with this. Prince Shotoku (574–622), who ruled as regent of Japan from 593 onwards, was a devout Buddhist and is believed to have owned two recently re-polished swords preserved by the Shitennoji Temple in Osaka. These specimens' crystalline structure shows that at this time the Japanese sword was already beginning to acquire some of its characteristic forms, particularly through being forged from different grades of steel.

The founding in 710 of Nara, Japan's first permanent capital city – and a miniature version of the Tang-dynasty capital of Chang'an (modern Xi'an) – was a major step forward in the governance of Japan. The Nara Period was a time of stability, and from this time several fine swords have survived. This is largely due to the creation of the Shosoin, a remarkable

The figure on the right of this group – from a modern copy of the Gosannen War Scroll in the Gosannen War Memorial Museum at Gosannen, Akita Prefecture – is wearing armour in the *yoroi* style. His *tachi* hangs down from his belt, together with a shorter dagger-like weapon and a wooden ring for a spare bowstring.

imperial storehouse built in Nara to house the personal effects of Emperor Shomu, who died in 756. Thousands of royal treasures in perfect condition are still in the Shosoin; this includes 55 swords. The Nara Period style of sword is characterized by a straight blade made more solidly than the earlier types through having a pronounced ridge (*shinogi*) running the length of the blade on one side. Later Japanese swords would have a *shinogi* on both sides.

The making of fine swords was an activity that flourished within the ordered world provided by Chinese-style bureaucracy – another great gift from the Asian mainland adopted by Japan. This bureaucracy included an army based on a system of conscription, with the army's warlike energies chiefly expended at the geographical extremities of Nara rule. In the south and west of Japan forts were garrisoned against a possible invasion from Korea, following the defeat of Japan's ally Baekje. In the north and east the Nara armies combated the *emishi*, the northern aboriginal tribes that challenged the growing domination of the Yamato court (the fledgling imperial power took its name from that of Yamato province, in Nara Prefecture). The *emishi* were regarded by the Yamato rulers as barbarians. However, it is possible that it is to them that we owe the most important development in Japanese sword technology: the introduction of the curved blade. This appears to have originated around 794, when the imperial capital was moved from Nara to Heian-kyo (modern Kyoto). Quite why the curve developed, and under what influences, is still a matter of dispute.

This hanging scroll in Himeji Castle, Hyogo Prefecture, depicts Sakai Tadahiro (1777–1837). Here we see a sword worn in katana style, with the cutting edge uppermost. The weapon's short length and the fact that it is being worn indoors suggest the sword is a *wakizashi*.

One theory is that the curved blade derived from the edged weapons used by the *emishi*, who used curved blades very effectively from the saddle against Nara's infantry-based armies. The argument goes that over the years the conscript armies of Nara were replaced by mounted warriors – the first samurai, who adopted this crucial element of military technology. With a lessening of Chinese influence and a flowering of Japanese swordmaking techniques, the new style of mounted warfare demanded a weapon that was better for slashing than for thrusting, so the classic Japanese sword was born. However, one weakness of this theory is that examples of swords found in north-eastern Japan could as easily be regarded as evidence of transmission to the *emishi* as from them. Also, the supposed advantages to a mounted warrior of a curved blade apply equally to a warrior on foot. In fact, one might even argue that the straight-bladed *chokuto*, with its sharp point and keen cutting edge, would provide the ideal cavalryman's sword, allowing the rider to run an infantryman through as well as cutting at him.

An alternative theory sees the curved blade originating simply as a fortuitous 'spin-off' from the process described above, whereby the cutting edge and the body of a sword were selectively hardened. Temperature differentiation would mean the process would naturally produce a slight curve in the blade; the clever *tosho* would not attempt to eradicate this but would instead exploit it for aesthetic and practical reasons.

The term *tachi* is conventionally applied to these early curved swords, which were worn slung from a belt with the cutting edge downwards. It is therefore unfortunate that so few specimens of early *tachi* have survived to provide a record of evolution. One reason for this is that during the Medieval Period many of these fine long blades were deliberately shortened so they could be worn more conveniently in katana style, with the cutting edge uppermost. As the shortening was done from the tang end such specimens would often lose the signature of their makers, leaving only their provenance or other anecdotal evidence to date them. One of the earliest curved blades to have survived intact is the sword called *Kogarasu-maru* ('Little Crow') – an heirloom of the Taira family that is now in the imperial collection. This is already in the recognizable *tachi* style. The curve of the blade is deep towards the hilt end and less so towards the point and a *shinogi* now appears on both sides of the blade.

Early *tachi* and their mountings were beautiful objects. The fittings were often works of art in their own right, with wooden scabbards covered in leather and beautifully lacquered and with gilt ornaments. Small carved metal fittings (*menuki*) lay on top of the *same*, bound in tightly by silken cords – traditional decorative features still found to this day. Here we see immense development in native swordmaking. Whereas the swords found in the *kofun* mounds tended to be imported from China, by the late Heian Period the quality of Japanese swords was so well known that trade was being conducted in the reverse direction. We can read of Japanese swords being praised by connoisseurs from the Song dynasty as 'treasure swords', with which one could 'defeat barbarians'.

The curved swords of such times began the period of *Koto*, a conventional expression meaning 'Old Swords' that lasts up to 1600, after which time we find *Shinto* or 'New Swords'. The Koto Period of swordmaking is conveniently approached through five main styles called the Five Traditions, each associated with a particular pre-modern Japanese province. The Yamato tradition is the most ancient, and takes its name from the emergence of Yamato province as the political centre of the Yamato court – the powerful lineage that would become the imperial house of Japan.

Yamato's legendary first swordsmith was Amakuni, who is said to have lived during the eighth century. Among the pieces attributed to him is the sword '*Kogarasu-maru*'. Nearby Yamashiro province (Kyoto Prefecture) contained the city that had succeeded Nara as capital of Japan. This province produced the early swordsmith Sanjo Munechika, who had several distinguished followers. In Sagami (Soshu, now Kanagawa Prefecture) province, the later capital of Kamakura was located from 1192 onwards. Kamakura became the seat of the shogun, the military dictator of Japan whose power eclipsed imperial rule, and under the patronage of successive shoguns several swordsmiths produced outstanding work. In 1249 the swordsmith Awataguchi Kunitsuna from Yamato forged a sword for the regent Hojo Tokiyori, and Kunitsuna's son Shintogo Kunimitsu continued the tradition from the new base in Sagami. His son in turn became the teacher of Masamune, one of the greatest swordmakers of all time.

Bizen province (Okayama Prefecture) on the Inland Sea owed its swordmaking tradition not directly to imperial or military patronage but to the fortuitous presence of iron sand in its riverbeds. The availability of this natural resource was to continue until disastrous floods during the sixteenth century removed much of the deposit. By that time many fine swords had been produced, particularly around the town of Osafune. However, the increased demand for swords during the fifteenth century, including many for export to China, led to Bizen also becoming a centre for the mass production of inferior weapons. Such production was also true of the swordsmiths belonging to the fifth of the Five Traditions, Mino (Gifu Prefecture). The Mino tradition began with a swordsmith who travelled there from Yamato. Production in Mino was centred on the town of Seki.

THE INTRODUCTION OF THE KATANA

From the later twelfth century onwards we can identify the emergence of the katana style. As noted, this had less to do with how the sword was forged and more with how it was mounted and used. Nowadays swords are classified as either *tachi* or katana depending on which side of the tang contains the maker's signature. This is because the signature was traditionally carved onto the side of the tang on the outside of the sword when it was being worn. Therefore a katana had the signature on the opposite side of the tang from the *tachi*.

Gaining an understanding of how the katana was introduced is bedevilled by the use of specialist terminology. Modern students and connoisseurs now use the words *tachi*, *katana*, *wakizashi* and *tanto* to identify various types of Japanese edged weapons, but these terms have more to do with classifying swords on artistic grounds. A *wakizashi* is a short sword that, together with a katana, makes up a *daisho* – a pair of swords furnished with identical mounts and fittings. A *tanto* is a shorter-bladed weapon; the term is usually translated as 'dagger'. Historically, it is better to approach the subject from the viewpoint of what was actually worn at a samurai's side, where one would find one long sword in a slung scabbard and at least one other secondary edged weapon, used for purely practical purposes, worn in the belt. The 'companion side-arms' (using modern terminology) are either *wakizashi* or *tanto*. It was long believed that *wakizashi* were worn beside a katana when one was in everyday dress, while a *tanto* was worn only when armoured. However, an examination of contemporary portraits calls this assumption into question. A famous

Here we see an ornate example of the matching pair of katana and *wakizashi* known as a *daisho*. This was the effectively the 'badge of office' of a samurai and the symbol of his authority.

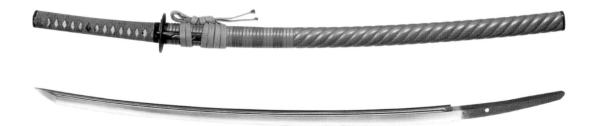

hanging scroll depicting Honda Tadakatsu (1548–1610) in armour shows him wearing not one but two companion swords that look like the conventional *wakizashi* and *tanto*. The *wakizashi* is worn on his left side and the *tanto* on his right. In contrast, a painted scroll of his contemporary Naito Ienaga (1546–1600), who died at the siege of Fushimi during the Sekigahara campaign, shows him in armour wearing a short-bladed weapon as his companion arm, and also with a long sword worn katana-style. Quite clearly, there were no hard and fast rules about how many weapons should be worn or how they should be carried.

An excellent example of a katana. *Menuki* (ornaments) are tightly bound onto the *tsuka* (handle) by silken cords. A small *kogai* (skewer) fits into a slot on the side of the beautifully carved scabbard. A *kozuka* (utility knife) would be found on the opposite side. Pictured below is the blade of a katana.

Naito Ienaga (1546–1600), who died at the siege of Fushimi during the Sekigahara campaign, was a retainer of Tokugawa Ieyasu. This hanging-scroll portrait of him, housed in the Naito Museum, Nobeoka City, Miyazaki Prefecture, shows him in armour with a sword worn in katana style and with a shorter weapon.

21

When a *tachi* was worn, purely practical considerations dictated that the act of drawing the sword and delivering a blow were usually two distinct operations. The katana style, with the sword thrust into the belt with the cutting edge uppermost, allowed these two actions to be combined in one devastating whole. The first use of the word *katana* to indicate the presence of a long weapon that differed from a *tachi* appears about the end of the twelfth century. At this time we come across the terms *uchigatana* and *tsubagatana* (these are compounds having the word *katana* as the second element; the 'k' sound has become a 'g' between vowels in the compound form). The second of the alternative terms, *tsubagatana*, has the first element *tsuba* ('sword guard'); such guards are always found on the *tachi*. For a warrior of modest means this shorter, less ornate weapon would simply have been a 'poor man's *tachi*' – as is implied by a very valuable pictorial source dating from the end of the twelfth century. This is the picture scroll called *Ban Dainagon ekotoba*. It depicts an incident that occurred in 866 when the courtier Ban Dainagon burned down the Otenmon gate in the imperial palace compound. The scroll shows the deeds of that night being carried out by people dressed in the costumes of the late twelfth century – the time at which the scroll was painted, by Tokiwa Mitsunaga – rather than those of the ninth century. In one scene we see the unfortunate Ban Dainagon being punished for his crime by being exiled to Izu province. He is on his way there in an oxcart, escorted by officials and warriors. All but two of the men attending him wear swords, and two figures in particular clearly have these swords thrust into their belts with the blades uppermost in what was to become known as the katana style.

The *Ban Dainagon ekotoba* was created at the time of Japan's great civil war, known as the Gempei War (1180–85), which resulted in the establishment of the position of shogun, and the relegation of the emperor to a largely ceremonial and ritual function. The shogun was based at Kamakura, hence the use of the term 'Kamakura Period' to cover the period from 1192 to 1333. This was an age of great advances in swordmaking, and one that witnessed a unique example of royal patronage. In 1221 the retired emperor Go-Toba attempted to lead a coup to restore imperial power. Go-Toba's revolt against the shogunate was a failure and he was exiled to the island of Oki, where at least he could immerse himself in his great passion: the Japanese sword. Over a period of several years Go-Toba invited eminent swordmakers to visit his island. These men made some very fine swords during this remarkable period of imperial favour, with Go-Toba joining in several projects. The involvement of and encouragement by Go-Toba did much to make the Japanese sword appreciated as a work of art as well as a weapon.

As the centuries went by the samurai grew to prefer the katana style over the *tachi*. Using just the criterion of the location of the signature, long swords intended for wearing as katana rather than slung *tachi* began to be made from about 1400 onwards. There is a parallel here to the evolution of Japanese armour, with the box-like *yoroi*-style armour of the twelfth-century mounted warrior giving way to the closer-fitting *do-maru* or *haramaki* originally worn by lower-class warriors. The impetus for both developments is usually explained as the increased incidence of fighting on foot during the Nambokucho Wars (the 'Wars between the Courts') of the fourteenth century. More neatly designed armour and swords worn in the belt would have been advantageous in the long series of small-scale sieges that characterized this conflict. It is more than likely that the samurai began the trend by wearing their precious *tachi* as katana; when after a time this became the norm, swordsmiths would respond by placing their signatures on the opposite side of the tang. However, it is important to note that the reverse choice could also be made – to wear a katana in *tachi* style. This may well be the case in the picture of Honda Tadakatsu discussed above, because combinations of leather pads and cords existed that allowed the sword to sit securely against armour in a horizontal position. In such a case the only way to tell whether the sword was a *tachi* or a katana would be to examine the position of the signature.

The number of swordsmiths known to us by name grows from about 450 in the Heian Period to 1,550 in the Kamakura Period. The battles against the Mongol invaders in 1274 and 1281 underscored the superiority of the Japanese sword over its Chinese-type counterpart until, with the Nambokucho Wars, sword regularly clashed with sword in domestic conflicts. It is also around the time of the Nambokucho Wars that we note the emergence of much longer-bladed swords. The extra-long sword, with the blade also wider than a normal *tachi* or katana, was known as the *odachi* or *nodachi*. Such weapons could not be worn at the waist and had to be carried on the samurai's back, so were also known as the *seoidachi* ('back-carried *tachi*'). These are frightening-looking weapons, seemingly capable of rendering enormous damage to a man or horse when employed by a warrior with the strength and skill to wield them. Displayed in a museum or a shrine, they are no less impressive. However, many of the surviving specimens were in fact made for presentation as a votive offering to a shrine or temple rather than for actual use on the battlefield. They would simply have been too heavy to use.

As the fourteenth century gave way to the fifteenth the number of known active swordsmiths jumps to around 3,550, until with the widespread conditions of war in the Sengoku Period (conventionally dated 1467–1603), many swords were being mass-produced, with a consequent loss in artistic quality and an inevitable reduction in strength and durability. Records exist of swords being shipped in their thousands to China, with disputes arising over quality and price. However, there were still many instances where fine swordsmiths made fine blades. For a superior to present a war hero with a magnificent sword meant his expertise was valued and a wish to ensure his continued wellbeing, so to receive such a sword in this manner was a great honour.

Three sizes of sword are shown in this woodblock. The samurai has a *tachi* hung from his belt together with a shorter weapon, while across his back is slung a *nodachi* or *seoidachi* (literally a 'shoulder-sword').

THE KATANA FROM BLADE TO SCABBARD

KEY

1. *kissaki*: fan-shaped cutting tip; point
2. *boshi*: wave-pattern of the tip
3. *mune*: blunt, back edge of the blade
4. *hasaki*: cutting edge
5. *hamon*: wave pattern
6. *shinogi-suji*: the ridge running the length of the blade
7. *ji*: area between the ha and the shinogi
8. *shinogi-ji*: flat surface between the shinogi and the mune
9. *ha*: tempered edge of the blade
10. *munemachi*: notch dividing the tang and the mune
11. *hamachi*: notch dividing the tang and the ha
12. *mekugi-ana*: peg-hole
13. *nakago yasuri-me*: tang file-mark pattern
14. *mei*: signature
15. *nakago*: tang
16. *nakago-jiri*: butt of the tang
17. *fuchi*: metal sleeve at the end of the hilt
18. *tsuka-maki*: wrappings on the hilt
19. *same*, 'sharkskin'; actually the skin of a giant ray
20. *menuki*: decorative metal fitting placed under the hilt wrappings
21. *tsuba*: sword guard
22. *habaki*: metal collar around the blade, just below the guard
23. *kogai/kozuka*: skewer/small knife
24. *kurigata*, 'chestnut-shape': cord knob of scabbard
25. *sageo*: cord that passes through the kurigata
26. *saya*: scabbard
27. *koi-kuchi*, 'carp mouth': metal fitting at the end of the scabbard

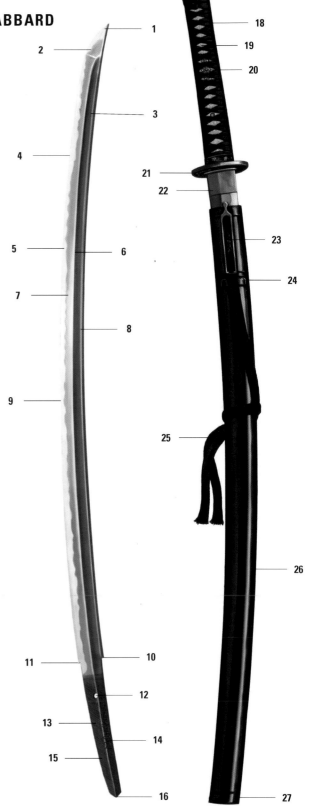

THE ARMOUR OF A SAMURAI

KEY

1. *kabuto*: helmet
2. *fukigayeshi*: helmet turnbacks
3. *mabisashi*: peak
4. *shikoro*: neck guard
5. *mempo*: face mask
6. *sode*: shoulder guards
7. *kote*: sleeve armour
8. *do*: body armour
9. *kusazuri*: tassets
10. *haidate*: thigh guards

Originally made for the Niwa family, this armour is of the Edo Period, and is a *mogami-do*, laced in the *sugake-odoshi* (spaced-out braid) style. Japanese armour was made from iron scales sewn together into strips and then lacquered, with the strips then tied together with silken cords to make an armour 'plate'. This meant that unlike a European suit of armour, Japanese armour would progressively absorb a blow, just like a modern flak jacket. The cords could of course be cut through quite easily, hence the frequent image in Japanese prints of a suit of armour cut to pieces, but if the armour retained its overall integrity it provided a very good defence.

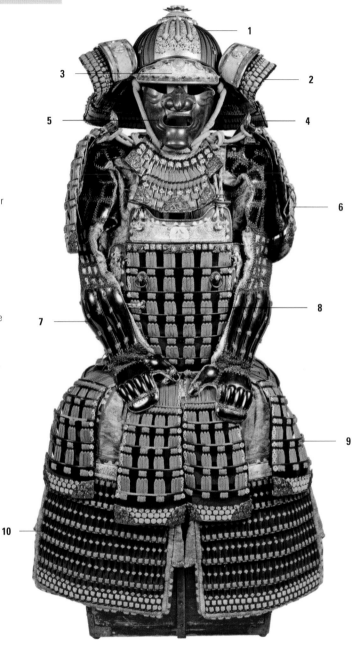

Every samurai on every battlefield of the Sengoku Period wore a sword. A spear may have been his primary weapon, but the sword was always there as his ultimate safeguard and his badge of rank. As for the size of a sword, much depended on the individual's own choice, as Matsudaira Chikuzen-no-kami commented concerning certain prominent generals of the late sixteenth century:

> Weapons are things that depend on a particular person's abilities and preferences. Kato Kiyomasa was above the common run of men and possessed a surpassing physical strength. He wore a large suit of armour with items of military use tied at his hips, and carried a *tachi* up to a *sun* [1in] in width. Kato Yoshiaki, he of the similar name, was a small man and was in fact a weak person. He wore leather armour and carried a 2 *shaku* [2ft] 1 *sun* narrow-bladed sword. However, Akai Hiza'emon of Shinshu was a weak little man but liked a heavy sword up to a *sun* in width. With this he once chased after a fleeing man, and cut him down from the top of his left shoulder to his right thigh.

THE KATANA IN THE AGE OF PEACE

With the decisive battle of Sekigahara in 1600, the Tokugawa family were confirmed as the rulers of Japan – a position they were to enjoy for two and a half centuries. Within a few years of the establishment of the Tokugawa shogunate, in the conditions of peace the standards of even 'one-off' swords began to decline. The old lore was lost, and unscrupulous swordmakers began to exploit the ignorance that affected so many of the samurai class. Two notorious names of the Shinto ('New-Swords') Period are Iga-no-kami Kanemichi and Tsuda Sukehiro. The former was granted the title of 'Chief Swordsmith of Japan' by Tokugawa Ieyasu, but used his position to sell certificates of competence to other, inferior smiths. A total of 910 swordsmiths are known to have purchased this spurious respectability. Tsuda Sukehiro went in for a personal version of mass production, churning out swords at the rate of five per month over a 25-year career.

Although the conditions of peace meant swords were not needed on the battlefield, this was also the golden age of the sword as a weapon of assassination and revenge. The story of the Loyal Retainers of Ako (the famous 'Forty-Seven Ronin') tells of the raid they conducted using swords with which they had spent many hours in secret training. On a snowy night early in 1703, the vengeful samurai, wearing protective armour that they had manufactured secretly, launched a raid on the mansion in Edo (modern Tokyo) belonging to the man they blamed for the death of their master. One of the fiercest swordfights of the Edo Period ensued, with much skill being shown on both sides.

Other encounters were of a more spontaneous nature. Rivals might be cut down in ambushes at crossroads, and there was also the constant possibility of swords being unsheathed during episodes of drunkenness or

慶応二年（長五郎四十七歳）

血煙荒神山

三州吉良吉司の仁吉に援を求む

清水党仁吉の義侠に組み三十人

月八日伊勢荒神山に穴徳

黒駒の徒と闘う浪人門之助を

七政小政で囲み大政の穂に倒す

死す仁吉の銃創に？

brawling. Nowhere was this more likely than in the teeming city of Edo, the Tokugawa shogun's capital. Here thousands of samurai dwelt in barracks assigned to their daimyo, who themselves had been forced to reside in Edo for a large part of every year. Swordfights with townsmen (who were often better armed and more highly skilled than the idle samurai) provided a headache for the keepers of the shogun's peace. Fights might break out over gambling debts or women, or even simply because of boredom. A notice issued by the shogun to the daimyo of Tosa made it clear that if a man was cut down outside their barracks he should be hunted down by the Tosa samurai, who were allowed to kill him if he did not surrender his sword.

Many samurai, forced to subsist on a fixed stipend and unable to gain promotion through the ranks by valiant conduct now that warring had ceased, found it difficult to maintain the traditional social status of which the katana was the badge. Some even took up trades to eke out their meagre income. This was greatly disapproved of by those who could afford to cling to the samurai tradition of battlereadiness and prowess in the martial arts. 'Only the swords through their belts remind them of their status,' wrote one appalled commentator, who was not aware that in some extreme cases poverty-stricken samurai had even pawned the blades of their swords and gone on guard duty with bamboo weapons inside their fine scabbards.

A depiction of the 1866 swordfight known as the 'Spray of Blood on Kojinyama', from the Shimizu Jirocho Memorial Museum, Shimizu City, Shizuoka Prefecture. The swordsman faces two assailants – one armed with a spear, the other with a sword.

27

Some samurai, however, did keep their skills and traditions alive through constant practice and attendance at the swordfighting academies run by master swordsmen. Towards the middle of the nineteenth century the keenest students in this regard tended to be drawn from the opposite extremes of the emerging political divide. The arrival of foreigners on Japan's sacred land had brought about a polarization of opinion. One faction sought to purge Japan of the 'pollution' brought by foreign visitors. Their rivals favoured the shogun's official policy of openness, and the anti-foreign element was the first to turn to the katana as an adjunct to politics. To cries of 'Honour the Emperor and expel the barbarians', the katana was wielded in a succession of attacks on the pro-foreign statesmen. In time this exclusionist sentiment grew to encompass a desire to overthrow the shogun and restore notional imperial power. Once the reality of this threat became apparent the shogun's response was equally ruthless. It resulted in some of the bloodiest swordfights seen off the battlefield in the whole of Japanese history. However, within a few years swords were again to be wielded on battlefields too. The year 1868 saw the Boshin War fought in northern Japan between imperial supporters and the last remnants of the shogun's army. When the territory of the Kubota fief (part of today's Akita Prefecture) was invaded by the army from Shonai (Yamagata Prefecture), the defenders collected weapons and armour from family storehouses; however, they were overwhelmed by the modern equipment of their rivals. But in the last battle at Kariwano the positions were reversed, and the defeated Shonai army, which had exhausted its ammunition supply and its soldiers in a battle that lasted all night, drew their katana for a final suicidal dawn attack.

The result of this brief civil war was to confirm the restoration of the emperor, but there was not to be the expulsion of foreigners that the Meiji government's original supporters had hoped for. Instead, with Western help Japan began to modernize, and when the country finally emerged on the international stage the wearing of swords was banned for all except members of the armed forces. No other decree so perfectly summed up the passing of the samurai. It was indeed the end of an era.

USE
Swordsmanship, battles and duels

THE *TACHI* IN SAMURAI WARFARE

Despite all the lore and tradition associated with the Japanese sword, it is important to remember that for many centuries the samurai was primarily a mounted archer – a notion borne out by contemporary literature and illustrations. First, there is not a single illustration of swords being wielded from horseback in any extant painted scroll or picture produced before the thirteenth century. Second, in literature too the samurai is primarily portrayed as an archer, as may be gathered from the earliest *gunkimono* (war tales). The latter are epic accounts of early samurai warfare, and from them many conclusions may be drawn about the values and ideals of the samurai in combat, even if these were rarely realized on the battlefield. *Shomonki* tells of the revolt of Taira Masakado, who was killed in battle in 940. Here there are only two references to the use of swords. The first may be purely metaphorical when it speaks of 'crossing swords with the enemy'. The other notes that Masakado is holding a sword as he rides into battle.

However, we must be careful not to take the notion of the mounted archer too far because it is just as difficult to find any artistic depiction of a samurai who does not have a sword hanging from his belt, and it would be unreasonable to assume that these fine weapons were simply there for decoration. The swords we see worn in picture scrolls such as *Heiji Monogatari emaki* (Picture Scroll of the Heiji Incident, which took place in 1160) are the *tachi* and the shorter weapon stuck into the belt around the waist of the armour. The shorter weapon (usually referred to as a 'dagger') was much easier to draw from its scabbard in the heat of battle than the two-handed *tachi*, and is frequently mentioned as being used to decapitate a defeated enemy who has been killed or mortally wounded by an arrow. Thus, Tomoe Gozen, the warrior woman who was the female

This print depicts Minamoto Yoritomo, the first shogun, as a young mounted warrior. Unusually, he is shown wielding a sword rather than a bow from the saddle. In this case the tactic has been effective because in a single-handed blow he has knocked his dismounted opponent's sword out of his hands.

companion-in-arms of Minamoto Yoshinaka, is described at the battle of Awazu in 1184 as pulling her victim out of his saddle and cutting off his head with her 'dagger'.

The *tachi* would come into its own when two rivals were dismounted and neither was particularly disadvantaged. In this scenario the *tachi* would be held in a two-handed grip and slashing strokes rather than stabbing movements would be the normal mode of operation. When the *tachi*'s use is described in *gunkimono* we note the use of verbs best translated as 'cut', 'strike' or 'slash'. In *Mutsu waki*:

> Before the words had left his mouth, he began to cleave a path through the centre of the enemy host, slashing right and left so savagely that no one ventured to face him. When he had killed three men, wounded six, and sustained innumerable wounds himself, he loosened his armour-belt, cut open his belly, and died on the same battlefield as his brother.

Wakiya Yoshisuke, who died in 1340, was the brother of Nitta Yoshisada, one of the great heroes of the Nambokucho Wars. Here he is shown bringing his *tachi* down with such force as to fracture the helmet his opponent is wearing. 'Helmet-breaking' was considered the toughest challenge to a blade and to a samurai's physical strength.

In comparison, when the short-bladed weapon is being described the verbs tend to be 'stab' and 'thrust' – consistent with the way the weapon was normally employed. In *Heike Monogatari* one young warrior is forcibly dismounted at the battle of Shinowara in 1183. He loses his bow and, coming to his senses, he draws his *tachi*:

> Arikuni, having penetrated very deeply into the ranks of the foe, had his horse shot from under him, and then while he was fighting on foot, his helmet was struck from his head, so that he looked like a youth fighting with his long hair streaming in all directions. By this time his arrows were exhausted, so he drew his sword and laid about him mightily until, pierced by seven or eight shafts, he met his death still on his feet and glaring at his enemies.

Holding his helmet in front of his face, a samurai facing a hail of arrows wields his *tachi* in a one-handed grip.

During the naval battle at Mizushima in 1183 Taira Noritsune stretched planks across ropes to make a solid platform for hand-to-hand combat. Arrows were used first, but swordplay followed on this artificial battleground:

> And so shouting their warcry they began the fight, drawing their bows and pouring in a hail of arrows until they came to close quarters, when they drew their swords and engaged each other hand to hand.

The wounds produced in such encounters could be dreadful, and one reason for the *tachi*'s horrible efficiency in killing was that the curvature of its blade allowed the very hard and sharp cutting edge to slice into an opponent along a small area, which would then open up as the momentum of the swing continued, cutting through to the bone. A samurai in *Taiheiki*, the great *gunkimono* of the Nambokucho Wars, draws his *tachi* and 'with one hand he brought down his sword, easily cut off Shichito's legs at the knees, and cast him three bows' lengths away'. When the blow delivered by a *tachi* was a two-handed one (as in normal usage), it possessed even greater energy. The katana could also act as a shield, thus providing an example (similar to that of the European rapier) of a sword used defensively as well as offensively. This defensive use depended upon the immense strength and resilience of the sword's body and its broad back, which enabled the samurai to deflect a blow aimed at him by knocking the attacking sword to one side with the flat of the blade and then following up with a stroke of his own.

Incidents off the battlefield provide other instances of fine swordplay against armed men. In *Gikeiki*, the youth Shanao – later to be called Minamoto Yoshitsune and a powerful general during the Gempei Wars – is caught up in a raid. The intruders note his delicate features and presume he is a girl – until he engages them in swordplay:

Two samurai of the Kamakura Period, armed with swords, appear on this hanging scroll in Toyama Castle Museum. The one on the left has a *tachi*, the one on the right an extra-long *nodachi* over his shoulder.

Out he flew at the intruders and scattered them with his sword. 'What a bold wench this girl is!' said Yuri Taro, turning back to meet Shanao. He took a step and swung with all his might, meaning to dispose of him with a single blow. He was a tall man, however, and the blade of his long sword stuck in the ceiling. As he struggled to extricate it, Shanao struck off his left arm, sleeve and all, with his short sword. With a second blow Shanao took his head.

Yuri Taro's comrade then attacks Shanao with a *naginata* (a curved-bladed polearm), only to have the shaft of his weapon cut in two and his helmet and face split open. To cut into the metal of a helmet bowl, the strongest part of a samurai's suit of armour, would test a sword blade to its limits. The ability of a Japanese sword to do this relied as much on the ability of its resilient inner core to withstand shock and bending as it did on the super-hard cutting edge. 'Helmet-breaking' was also considered the supreme trial for the

33

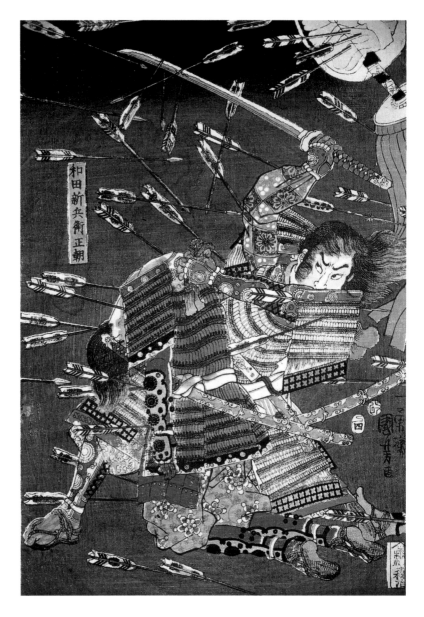

swordsman's physical strength, and it was said that the samurai Maehara
Chikuzen-no-kami could 'smash a sixty-two plate helmet' – a reference to
a popular design of helmet, made from a series of curved overlapping plates
riveted together.

Not every katana could take such extreme punishment. In the pressure
to produce enough swords to supply an army's needs, quality could be
sacrificed for the sake of quantity. There are several references to swords
being broken or damaged either in clashes with other swords or when
struck against resistant surfaces such as the heavy iron of a helmet.
However, a high-ranking samurai would have attendants who could
supply him with replacement swords should his own break. In *Taiheiki*,
Nagasaki Takashige seems very pragmatic about possible failings in both

swords and horses, because 'when his horse was wearied, he mounted a new one; when his sword was broken, he put a new one at his waist'. Later in the same chapter we read how he overcomes a horse and its rider with one mighty blow:

> He put Shigesane on his left side and split his helmet bowl down to the cross-stitched lower flap, so that Shigesane was cleft in two and perished. Likewise Shigesane's horse, its knee cut, was knocked over backwards in a heap.

Sometimes a sword would get stuck, embedded in an opponent's body. This could have serious consequences for the victor, who now had nothing to defend himself with against other opponents; hence, prayers existed for swords to be dislodged. A sword could also become wedged when a well-made suit of armour successfully provided the protection for which it was designed by absorbing the blow over several layers. One armoured samurai survived 13 cuts to his body, while the grave pits of Zaimokuza, which contain the remains of victims of the capture of Kamakura by Nitta Yoshisada in 1333, show very clearly the comparative effects of the Japanese sword on unprotected bodies. Many of the bodies are of civilians, and slash wounds to limbs and skull appear on 60 per cent of the male skeletons, 30 per cent of the female skeletons and ten per cent of the children. Most cuts were to the forehead or top of the head, suggesting they were delivered by mounted men. Some blows must have had considerable force, because in certain cases the blade has bounced and cut again, or the skull has simply been crushed.

JAPANESE SWORDS AND THE MONGOL INVASIONS

The first opportunity for native Japanese swords to be tested against the Chinese models they had replaced came with the attempted Mongol invasions of 1274 and 1281. Here, during boat-borne raids against the Mongol fleet, swords rather than bows proved to be of the greatest practical use. At about this time sword technology was reaching its point of perfection, and the opportunities for hand-to-hand combat rather than arrow exchange at a distance provided the perfect test. The long, curved, razor-sharp blades cut deeply into the brigandine-like coats of the Mongol invaders, whose short swords were much inferior. The contrast in weaponry was to be noted frequently during the raids by 'little ships'. Kawano Michiari led a daytime raid with two boats, accompanied by his uncle Michitoki and five followers. The Mongols, thinking the Japanese were coming to surrender, allowed them to come close, at which point the mast was let down and the Mongol ship was boarded. Michiari's uncle Michitoki was killed instantly by an arrow, while Michiari was wounded first in the shoulder and then in the left arm by catapult missiles. However, on boarding the ship Michiari's swordplay led to the death of a huge Mongol warrior and the capture of a high-ranking general.

Another samurai who engaged in such raiding recommended to his followers that they first hook the Mongols at a distance using *kumade* (bear-paw polearms), and when the enemy were immobilized a sword blade should be slid through the joints of their armour. This pragmatic approach was a far cry from the image of the samurai swordsman squarely facing an honourable opponent, but in a situation where a samurai's prowess was measured by the number of severed enemy heads he took back to his commander the notion of 'honourable' one-to-one swordsmanship was quietly abandoned. Many years later, at the battle of Sekigahara in 1600, a retainer of Nagatsuka Masaie armed himself with a long-handled rake with multiple prongs. With this he entangled opponents, which let his attendants quickly finish them off with swords. Of course it was Nagatsuka Masaie, not his followers, who was credited with their heads.

The defeat of the Mongols, in part due to the superiority of the Japanese sword, made a point that was not lost on contemporary Chinese scholars, two of whom made specific reference to the weapon. The early fourteenth century Chinese scholar Zheng Sixiao (1241–1318) was very wary of the Japanese pirates who raided China and Korea. He wrote that they were 'fierce and do not fear death' and that ten Japanese soldiers would fight an enemy unit of 100 men. He also made a particular reference to Japanese swords, writing that 'their swords were extremely sharp'. Huang Zhencheng (1287–1362) described a Japanese pirate raid as 'a multitude of dancing butcher knives'. Later descriptions are in a very similar vein, as for example in the *Riben kao* of Ye Xiangga: 'They disdain life and are bloodthirsty… The blades of the Japanese swords are sharp. Chinese swords are inferior.' For this reason Japanese swords found a ready market on the Asian mainland, and ships containing thousands of blades made their way to China at the time of the internationally minded shogun Ashikaga Yoshimitsu in the late fourteenth century.

THE SWORD ON THE SENGOKU BATTLEFIELD

The nature of battlefield swordplay, which required adequate space for the sword to be wielded effectively, meant swords were used less than spears within the tightly packed ranks of samurai typical of the ordered layout of a Sengoku Period battle. Swordplay would typically occur later in the course of battles, when relative disorder meant those who fought were more widely spaced out. The swordsman in action on the sixteenth-century battlefield therefore became the individual warrior he always believed himself to be, even though circumstances may have dictated that this would not happen very often. Fighting was often done on foot with horses kept at the rear ready for a pursuit. This may have been for purely tactical reasons, as at Osaka in 1615, but some horses were frightened by the sight of sword blades and on occasions samurai were thrown by horses that had been startled in such a way by riders' or enemies' swords. Conversely a sword, particularly an extra-long *nodachi* in the hands of an enemy on foot, could pose a severe threat to a mounted man. Most likely the horse would be the primary target, with the animal brought down by cutting against its legs. Some of these longer swords were not sharpened near the hilt and could be used as a club as well as a cutting weapon.

Swords were much more often used during sieges; an example is Kamiizumi Nobutsuna's swordplay at Minowa. The sword expert Kamiizumi led a sally out of the rear gate into the midst of the Takeda enemy. Toyotomi Hideyoshi's invasions of Korea in 1592 and 1597 also saw a great deal of siege warfare. Much of the fighting involved mass use of arquebus and spear, but occasionally we find accounts of swordplay that provided further opportunities for Japanese swords to be compared with their mainland counterparts. It was noted how Japanese swords cut deeply into the armoured coats of China's Ming soldiers, and when the Japanese captured Namweon in 1597 some fierce swordfighting took place.

Oda Nobunaga makes good use of his katana when trapped within Honnoji Temple by Akechi Mitsuhide. This incident in 1582 led to Nobunaga's death.

The siege of Namweon was the first major action on land as part of the second Japanese invasion of Korea. The Japanese piled up bundles of grass and straw beneath the ramparts of the town, climbed the walls and dropped down into the alleyways and courtyards, swords in hand. A valuable eyewitness account exists in the form of a diary kept by Okochi Hidemoto, a retainer of Ota Kasuyoshi. A Japanese assault party under Hidemoto was faced with a counterattack by mounted men, yet even in all this confusion and danger the personal credit for taking a head was all-important. Okochi Hidemoto was armed with a katana, and cut up towards the right side of the groin of an enemy who towered above him on horseback. The cut sank home, causing the rider to fall off his horse on the left-hand side, away from Okochi. There were some samurai standing nearby and three of them struck at the fallen enemy so as to take his head. Even though other enemies were nearby Okochi came running around so that he would not be deprived of the vital trophy.

Nearby a bizarre encounter took place between a group of Japanese and a giant 7ft-tall Korean swordsman. The latter was dressed in a black suit of armour, and as he swung his long sword a samurai thrust his spear towards the man's armpit, only to catch his sleeve instead. At the same time another Japanese warrior caught the man's other sleeve with his spear, ensuring the giant was now pinioned helplessly. He continued to swing his sword arm ineffectively from the elbow, as reported by one eyewitness, 'as if with the small arms of a woman,' but the reduction of this once-formidable foe drew only scorn from Okochi. Caught by two spears, and waving his arms pathetically, he reminded Okochi of the statues of Deva kings in Buddhist temples with their muscular bodies and glaring eyes. Facing contempt and ridicule from his attackers, the helpless giant was cut to pieces by Okochi's katana.

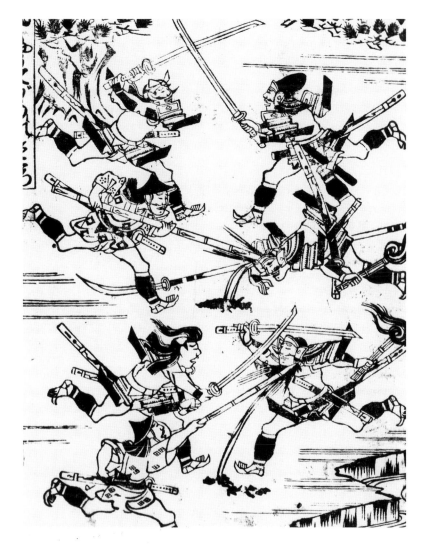

Okochi Hidemoto then came under attack himself. A group of Koreans cut at him and he was knocked to the ground. As he was getting up several more swordcuts were delivered to his chest, leaving him crouching on the ground gasping for breath. His comrade Koike Shinhachiro came to his aid while Hidemoto himself parried five swordstrokes with the edge of his blade. His katana was certainly well made and absorbed the punishment for which the resilient core was designed. Yet he failed to parry a sixth slash which struck home, cutting clean in two the middle finger of his bow hand. Enraged and weary, Okochi somehow managed to rise to his feet and quickly decapitated his assailant. Advancing more deeply into Namweon's alleys, Hidemoto encountered another strongman dressed magnificently in a fine suit of armour set off with dark blue cloth. He was clearly a high-ranking officer, as shown also by the presence of bodyguards. Hidemoto was cut in four places on his sleeve armour, and also received two arrows that penetrated deeply into his bow arm in two places, but despite these wounds he managed to overcome the man and take his head.

THE KATANA AND THE *KENGO*

Even though the nature of the Sengoku Period battlefield may have allowed little opportunity for individual swordplay, this was nonetheless the golden age of swordfighting. For most examples, however, we have to look away from the battlefield. Nowhere are the skills associated with using the katana, and passing on its traditions to others, better illustrated than through the lives of the handful of superlative swordsmen who lived at this time. The title given to them was *kengo* ('swordmaster'), and they contributed to the development of sword technique in several ways.

The first was through the example they gave to others that showed the sword's potential through actual fights. All *kengo* would have had considerable experience of serving in a daimyo's army and would have had several 'kills' to their credit, but the occasions that were most celebrated – and where their use of the katana was regarded as existing on a higher plane – took place away from the battlefield. These contests came about through duels and challenges, sometimes to the death, when the method of killing an opponent became almost an art form. Dramatic new techniques originated with particular *kengo*, whose skill and devotion to their art made experimentation both a possibility and an acceptable risk.

The *kengo* also contributed to the lore and the mystique of the Japanese sword via their writings and via conversations with devoted followers. The resulting spiritual insights were seen to link the katana to the wider world of Japanese religion – including, but not exclusively, Zen Buddhism – and provided a whole new dimension to the art of the swordsman. These practical techniques and philosophical discoveries would then be disseminated through society in two ways. The first was quite haphazard and came about when the *kengo* undertook a *musha shugyo* ('warrior's pilgrimage'). This was a journey undertaken to provide challenges with other swordsmen or to gain insight from spiritual leaders; such an activity has been harnessed in modern times to provide the classic image beloved of the movie industry, whereby a master swordsman wanders from place to place accepting challenges, defeating opponents and honing his skills.

Through these encounters a master swordsman developed a corpus of individual yet transferable skills that would become known as his *ryuha* or school. The term *ryuha* (shortened to -*ryu* when used as a suffix) can also have the meaning of 'style', and is best understood in the sense of a continuing tradition – like the 'School of Rembrandt' (as regards actual buildings, the Japanese equivalent of a school in martial arts terms is *dojo*, or 'practice hall'). One of the earliest swordfighting schools datable with some accuracy is the *Tenshin Shoden Shinto-ryu*, in which Tsukuhara Bokuden, our outstanding subject in the section which follows, was first trained. The school's founder, Iizasa Choisai Ienao, was probably born in 1387 and served the shogun Ashikaga Yoshimasa (1435–99) before returning to his home province. After many spiritual experiences associated with the Katori Shrine (which enshrined Futsunushi-no-kami, a martial arts *kami*), he founded the school which still exists to this day. Its association with the shrine explains its alternative name: the *Katori Shinto-ryu*.

Futsunushi, the martial-arts *kami* at Katori Shrine in Chiba Prefecture. This depiction of the martial deity shows him dressed as a Chinese general.

The second means of transmission came about when a *kengo* ceased or interrupted his wanderings to be hired by a powerful daimyo as *sensei* ('teacher') of the lord's own samurai. Note that the English translation of *sensei* as 'teacher' fails to do justice to the immense respect and authority vested in the term. The hiring of a *kengo* as a *sensei* could also result in the creation of a *ryuha* associated exclusively with that particular daimyo. In this section we will examine examples of the wanderer and the teacher in the person of four outstanding swordmasters.

The first of these is Tsukahara Bokuden (1490–1571). Bokuden was one of the earliest and greatest *kengo*, and a statue of him now stands by the road leading to the great Kashima Shrine, which dominates the modern town of Kashimajingu in Chiba Prefecture east of Tokyo. The hill on which the shrine stands, inside a dark ancestral forest, is one of the few patches of high ground in this mysterious part of Japan. The land is crisscrossed by rivers and if one visits at the time of the annual flooding of the rice fields prior to the transplanting of seedlings the whole plain seems to be nothing but water, with elevated roads and farmhouses left as if stranded. This was Tsukahara Bokuden's birthplace, but like many of the great swordsmen of Japanese history his origins are shrouded in mystery. Tradition tells us that he was adopted into the Tsukahara family after having been trained as a swordsman by his real father. This man combined the professions of samurai and Shinto priest; the latter vocation was based at the Kashima Shrine, where was enshrined the spirit of Takemikazuchi, another *kami* of the martial arts. Kashima is also quite close to the celebrated Katori Shrine.

Bokuden's talent brought him to the notice of Tsukahara Tosa-no-kami, a swordsman who had studied under Iizasa Choisai Ienao in the Katori Shinto-ryu. Tosa-no-kami's son and heir died young, so he adopted the promising young Bokuden. At the early age of 17 Bokuden's adoptive father gave him permission to set out on his first *musha shugyo*, which was very successful, and among those Bokuden defeated was a renowned swordsman called Ochiai. Bokuden spared his life, but it was such a disgrace to Ochiai to have been defeated by this young upstart that he later lay in wait for Bokuden in order to murder him. On their second encounter Ochiai was killed by a rapid stroke of Bokuden's sword. Bokuden then had to take his place in the armies of the local daimyo of Awa province. We have no record of the locations of Bokuden's involvement on the battlefield, other than a note that he fought in nine engagements using a spear, the primary samurai weapon in that situation, and took 21 heads. Of these seven were classified as *yarishita* (killed at the start of the battle, thus implying that Bokuden was in the front ranks of the samurai spearmen), *kuzuregiwa* (a kill made while covering a retreat, a very dangerous position) or *banaka* (a head taken at the height of the battle).

By the age of 37 Tsukahara Bokuden had developed his own unique style of swordfighting, which he named *Shinto-ryu*. This was an interesting choice of name because it was a homophone of the title of the school in which he had been trained. However, the Kanji ideograms for this version of the word *Shinto* were different from that used for the Tenshin Shoden Shinto-ryu, and translated as 'new strike'. The great secret of Bokuden's own art of swordsmanship was summarized in the mysterious expression '*hitotsu no tachi*' ('one stroke'), although the exact meaning of this is now lost to history. Judging from descriptions of Bokuden in action, the technique is unlikely to be simply that of delivering a deadly swordstroke directly from the scabbard. Bokuden did not claim that the technique was his own idea: he readily acknowledged that he had acquired it from another great master, Matsumoto Bizen-no-kami. A later document hints at the essence of the style in the following mystical language:

Tsukahara Bokuden, one of the earliest and greatest of the *kengo*, is shown here in a statue which stands by the road leading to the Kashima Shrine in Chiba Prefecture.

Hitotsu no tachi can be divided into the three levels... The first uses the timing of heaven. The second uses the vantage of the earth and is the move that unites heaven and earth. The third secret technique teaches harmony of man and innovation.

Timing would therefore appear to be of the essence, and in a later interpretation published in 1727 we find further clues that make the *hitotsu no tachi* technique reminiscent of the stock movie image of the swordsman eyeing up his opponent from a position of Zen-like detachment:

A swordsman must first position himself directly opposite his opponent's sword. He can place his sword either aloft before him or at his side. The only essential point is that he must look unprotected, provoking his opponent into a conventional attack.

From this passage we must conclude that the sword has already been drawn and is in the master's hands. A further dimension of the technique is then revealed. This involves calculating precisely the crucial distance between the opponents' swords:

If the opponent's sword is more than one inch away from his body, the swordsman should not parry his attack. When the sword is only half an inch away, however, the swordsman should take one step forward and slay his opponent.

The document goes on to stress the point that the essential skill was the ability to judge this distance precisely. Human nature would tend to make anyone try to avoid an incoming stroke, but if the master swordsman had judged the distance correctly he had nothing to fear because he knew for certain that the enemy's blade would not make contact with him. Being therefore completely relaxed about his defensive needs, the master swordsman's correct response is to put all his energy into attacking, which is the last thing that his opponent will expect.

An early practical application of this theory came about when Bokuden encountered a man called Kajiwara Nagato-no-suke, who was renowned for his wielding of the *naginata* – the long polearm with a curved blade popular among lower-class fighters in the Heian Period. A *naginata* was an unusual choice for a samurai of the Sengoku Period, when straight spears were their common polearm, but Nagato-no-suke had trained for years with this fierce weapon. The great advantage possessed by a skilled *naginata* fighter over a swordsman was that its long shaft enabled him to attack the swordsman at a distance which the sword could not cover. Bokuden anticipated this, and began the duel by concentrating on the blade of the *naginata* as if it were a katana held by a man closer to him than was the case. Judging his distance precisely, Bokuden delivered a rapid blow from the scabbard at the *naginata* as if he were cutting at this invisible opponent, and with this first stroke he sliced the shaft in half, leaving Nagato-no-suke defenceless. Bokuden then moved forward for a quick kill. It was a significant victory.

OPPOSITE

In this print a samurai is
holding his katana using the
recommended two-handed grip.

Tsukahara Bokuden's reputation grew rapidly, and while on his second *musha shugyo* he was invited to Kyoto to teach sword techniques to the shogun Ashikaga Yoshiteru (1535–65) – as great a commission as any *kengo* could receive. The family of Ashikaga ruled Japan as shoguns from 1333 until 1573, but the later members have often been represented as mere pawns in a power game, unable to stand up against the new daimyo who ruled petty kingdoms of their own, heedless of the shogun's authority. At the political level this is probably true, but thanks to Tsukahara Bokuden the Ashikaga family produced at least one skilled swordsman in the person of Yoshiteru, who became the 13th Ashikaga shogun in 1545 at the age of ten. Bokuden became his tutor in 1552, when Yoshiteru was 17 years old. Yoshiteru was a promising pupil, and his skills were put to their ultimate test in 1565 when rivals set out to get rid of him. At the time Yoshiteru was at his palace in Kyoto. In the middle of the night the palace was raided. The guards proved useless and Yoshiteru found himself surrounded on all sides. Guns were discharged into the room as Yoshiteru drew his sword and prepared to put into use the skills that Bokuden had taught him. His enemies appeared first only as dark shadows on the panels of the translucent paper screens that divided room from room. Sweeping the screens to one side to reveal his adversaries, Yoshiteru laid about them with the sword, using the skilled strokes of the Shinto-ryu. However, a spearman thrust at his legs and brought him to the ground. Mortally wounded by swordstrokes, Yoshiteru crawled into another room to commit suicide – a further noble gesture that gives the lie to the commonly held image of weak and effeminate shoguns.

Swordfighting postures from the *Heiho Okugisho*, attributed to Yamamoto Kansuke (1493–1561)

1. *Ukaketsuzen kennosei*: a defensive posture against an enemy who has his sword raised ready to cut downwards.

2. *Ukago kennosei*: an apparently casual posture favoured by the swordsman Sasaki Ganryu, who fought Miyamoto Musashi.

3. *Chudan*: a strong guard position with the sword held at medium height.

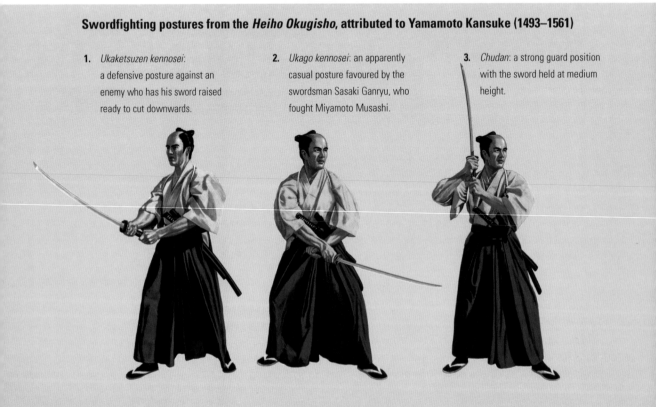

By the time Tsukuhara Bokuden went on his third *musha shugyo* his reputation had grown so much that he was attended by 80 followers and took along three spare horses. At the head of the procession he flew three hawks and he conducted himself as proudly as any daimyo. His procession was indeed splendid, but there was no false pride about Bokuden himself, for he realized, as did all great swordsmen, that no matter how good he was he needed to pass on his skills to one trusted follower if his school was to survive, and the warlike nature of the times made this very difficult. It is believed that the essential secrets of the *hitotsu no tachi* were passed on to Kitabatake Tomonori (1528–76), daimyo of Ise province and his trusted pupil. Like many *sensei*, Bokuden chose as his successor in the swordfighting arts someone who was not a member of his own family, but he did trust Tomonori to initiate Bokuden's son when the boy was old enough and worthy enough. Tomonori did indeed pass the knowledge on to Bokuden's youngest son, whom his father had named as his heir, but when Bokuden died in 1571 at the ripe old age of 81 his successors became the victims of forces far beyond the control of an individual swordsman. The Kitabatake suffered from the expansion into Ise province of Oda Nobunaga, and Tomonori died

4. *Sachu zenkennosei*: a threatening posture in which the swordpoint is aimed at the enemy's throat.

5. *Heijozen kennosei*: an unusual posture with the sword edge uppermost and supported by the left hand.

6. *Jodan no kamae*: a strong posture in which the sword is held ready to deliver a devastating downward stroke.

defending his territory. It is not clear whether he was killed on the battlefield or murdered by treacherous retainers, as accounts differ. Nor is anything known of the fate of Bokuden's son, apart from a few fascinating legends about him joining the ninja groups of Iga.

In spite of the lack of historical continuity, Tsukahara Bokuden remains a very important figure in the early history of the master swordsmen. Many stories are told about him. The best is undoubtedly his amusing but telling encounter with a boastful samurai on a ferryboat. The man in question had managed to terrify the other passengers with his bragging about his prowess at swordfighting. He then picked on the taciturn Bokuden, who alone had remained unintimidated, and challenged him to a fight. Bokuden politely declined, saying he never wielded his sword in such circumstances. The furious samurai poured scorn upon Bokuden for what he took to be cowardice. He asked Bokuden to name his school of swordfighting. Bokuden replied 'the *Munekatsu-ryu*' – 'the style that wins without a sword'. This made the samurai all the more angry, and he ordered the boatman to stop at a nearby island so he could teach the stranger a lesson. As they reached the island's beach the samurai leapt ashore and took up a guard position with his sword, screaming for Bokuden to disembark and fight him. At that moment Bokuden took the ferryman's pole and drove the boat away from shore, leaving the samurai stranded. To the samurai's yells of protest Bokuden shouted back to him: 'See, this is what I meant by the *Munekatsu-ryu*! After all, have I not just defeated you without drawing a sword?' This story is often told as a further example of the maxim encapsulated in the words of Tokugawa Ieyasu, to the effect that the sword is in its greatest position of strength while still lying in its scabbard.

This modern painting from Miyajima Municipal Museum shows samurai of the Mori in action on the island of Miyajima.

Whereas Tsukahara Bokuden's attempts at passing on his teaching to a worthy successor were somewhat frustrated by circumstances, there are other examples in which transmission was more successful and a long-lasting school was established. The need for this was linked to the realities of combat, because achieving success with a sword in the uncontrolled world of the battlefield (even for the warrior merely to survive) needed years of practice in the controlled environment of peacetime swordplay. Such activities, which involved practice, study and great dedication, were provided and mentored by a daimyo's *sensei*.

One important school of swordfighting that still exists in a modified form through its various offshoots is the *Kage-ryu* ('Shadow School'). This is associated particularly with the celebrated *kengo* Kamiizumi Nobutsuna, although he is not recognized as its actual founder. Kamiizumi Nobutsuna was as famous for his swordfighting experiences on the battlefield as for his wanderings. He helped defend Minowa Castle against the Takeda, and when it surrendered he was taken into the service of Takeda Shingen. Kamiizumi Nobutsuna's version of the Kage-ryu was named by him the *Shinkage-ryu* ('New Shadow School'). From Nobutsuna's Shinkage-ryu derived the *Yagyu Shinkage-ryu*, which became the most influential school of swordsmanship in Tokugawa Japan following a fateful swordfight between a member of the Yagyu family and Kamiizumi Nobutsuna's own protégé.

Kamiizumi Nobutsuna defended Minowa Castle against the Takeda and was then taken into the service of Takeda Shingen. He became one of the finest *kengo*.

The Yagyu were a minor daimyo family with lands in the vicinity of Nara, and in the mid-fifteenth century they were embroiled in the struggles for territory and power that went on in this part of Japan as elsewhere. Their celebrated *kengo* Yagyu Muneyoshi participated in his first battle at the age of 16. His battles included one against warrior monks during which Muneyoshi received an arrow through his hand, but this does not seem to have affected his swordfighting prowess. A few years later he fought the famous duel that marked the beginning of the Yagyu Shinkage-ryu. The wandering Kamiizumi Nobutsuna, journeying on his *musha shugyo*, had been given a letter of introduction to the monk Inei, chief priest of the Hozo-In Temple of Nara. Inei was related to Yagyu Muneyoshi. Knowing the reputation of both men, Inei decided to bring them together, so a contest was arranged to take place at the Hozo-In. Nobutsuna was then 55 years old, while Muneyoshi was 20 years younger. We may imagine Muneyoshi's disappointment when he learned that his opponent was not to be the great Nobutsuna himself, but his

nephew Hikita Bungoro. A further surprise awaited Muneyoshi when he arrived, because Bungoro was not carrying a *bokuto* (the solid wooden practice sword) but what appeared to be a bundle of bamboo sticks bound together – the prototype *shinai*, now familiar from modern *kendo*.

Muneyoshi faced his rival holding his *bokuto*. Each watched the other, waiting for an unguarded moment. Then suddenly Bungoro struck. Muneyoshi ignored the blow and continued the duel, only to receive the *shinai* again. At this point Muneyoshi realized that he had come across a style of swordfighting superior to his own, and was about to acknowledge this when the master Kamiizumi Nobutsuna took the *shinai* from Hikida Bungoro and challenged Muneyoshi to a further duel. Muneyoshi took his guard, but the mere gesture of the challenge had beaten him. He threw his *bokuto* to the ground and knelt before Nobutsuna, begging to be taken on as his pupil. Nobutsuna consented, and the result of his teaching was to be the Yagyu Shinkage-ryu, one of the greatest schools of swordsmanship that Japan would ever see.

The next important event in the life of the *kengo* Yagyu Muneyoshi occurred in 1594, when the future shogun Tokugawa Ieyasu invited him to his mansion in Kyoto. Tokugawa Ieyasu was very interested in swords, swordsmanship and martial arts in general. Muneyoshi was accompanied by his son Munenori, and they gave such a fine display of swordsmanship that the enthusiastic Ieyasu took a wooden sword to try his skill against Muneyoshi. He brought the *bokuto* down against Muneyoshi's forehead, but before he knew what had happened Muneyoshi had dodged, deflected the blow and grabbed the sword by the hilt. He held Ieyasu by the left hand and made a symbolic punch to his chest. The sword had gone spinning across the room. This was Muneyoshi's demonstration of the technique he called *muto* (literally 'no sword'). Following this encounter Ieyasu asked the Yagyu to become the Tokugawa's sword instructors. Muneyoshi excused himself on the grounds of his age, but suggested that his son Munenori would make an excellent *sensei*, an offer Ieyasu gladly accepted. Muneyoshi died in 1606, by which time their pupil Tokugawa Ieyasu had become shogun. Yagyu Munenori continued serving the Tokugawa until the third-generation shogun Iemitsu, but on the death of Muneyoshi the *ryuha* split into the Owari and the Edo Yagyu Shinkage-ryu. There was much rivalry between the Edo and Owari schools over the years to come, partly over which branch represented the authentically transmitted tradition, and also over which was the best. Yet both recognized that all the secret techniques in the world could not avail a

Minowa Castle, 1564 (previous pages)

Accounts of swords in use on the battlefield are surprisingly few in number, largely because the samurai used spears first and swords second. However, this picture illustrates an authentic incident in 1564 in which the specialist swordsman and *kengo* Kamiizumi Nobutsuna led a sally out of the rear gate of Minowa Castle and laid into the Takeda samurai, some of whom had swords, others spears. The artist's interpretation is based on written descriptions of the action.

swordsman unless he practised his art. In this context the author of the 'samurai manual' of the seventeenth century, called *Hagakure*, writes of a dying *sensei*, who told his best disciple:

> I have passed on to you all the secret techniques of this school, and there is nothing left to say. If you think of taking on a disciple yourself, then you should practise diligently with the bamboo sword every day. Superiority is not just a matter of secret techniques.

THE *JIGEN-RYU* OF SATSUMA

Few schools of swordfighting are more closely associated with their surroundings than the *Jigen-ryu* of Satsuma province (modern Kagoshima Prefecture), which provides an excellent case study. Kagoshima was the seat of the Shimazu family, of Satsuma, at the most southerly tip of Japan's second main island of Kyushu. Helped partly by the remote geographical location, the Shimazu family maintained an amazing degree of independence throughout the time of civil wars to become the great survivors of medieval Japan. Even when defeated by Toyotomi Hideyoshi in 1587 as part of his successful programme of reuniting Japan, they were able to negotiate a settlement whereby they continued to rule Satsuma on Hideyoshi's behalf. Fewer than 20 years later their support of the losing side at the decisive battle of Sekigahara in 1600 still resulted in a similar deal whereby they remained as daimyo of Satsuma, instead of being moved to a new territory as happened with most other lords. The respect accorded to them by their conquerors derived partly from the practical necessity of governing a remote territory, but also from the long run of successful military operations the Shimazu had conducted. These had made them masters of almost the whole of Kyushu by the time of Hideyoshi's intervention in 1587. Part of the secret of their success was the quality of their swordsmanship, which was then under the control of the school known as the *Taisha-ryu*.

The school called the *Jigen-ryu* that was to replace the Taisha-ryu was founded by a Satsuma samurai called Togo Shigekata, who had trained in the Taisha-ryu from the age of seven. At the age of 13 this prodigy had used a dagger successfully to quell a brawl, and at the age of 18 he engaged in his first battle. This was the massacre at the Mimigawa in 1578, when the Shimazu neutralized the power of their rivals the Otomo, leaving thousands of Otomo warriors dead along the riverbank. At 20 Shigekata was initiated into the most closely guarded secrets of the Taisha-ryu when he received the *menkyo kaiden* ('secrets of the art') documents from the current *sensei*, Higashi Shinnojo. All the schools of swordsmanship claimed to possess their own specific and secret traditions known only to a very few people who maintained the monopoly of this secret knowledge. The above-mentioned Yagyu Munenori, heir to the secret lore of the Yagyu Shinkage-ryu, expressed this in the following way in his preface to *Heiho Kaidensho*:

Togo Shigekata, the founder of the Jigen-ryu of Satsuma.

The contents of those three volumes must not be released outside this family; however, this does not mean that our Way has to be completely concealed. To withhold the prescribed skills and theories in our *ryu* means to preserve the purity of our tradition, and to transmit them to students who are truly qualified. If these are never transmitted to others, then it is as if I had never written.

In this treatise Munenori uses the words *ie* ('family' or 'household') and *ryu* almost interchangeably, in a way that implies that he saw his students as his own children. In this extended-family system the eldest son did not necessarily have precedence on inheritance. Although Munenori had inherited leadership of the Edo Yagyu Shinkage-ryu from his father Muneyoshi, he still pointed out that the successor to the head of the school was required to be the best-qualified student:

The first volume of this book was called *Shinrikyo*, and outlined the entire contents which were directly transmitted to my deceased father from its founder Kamiizumi Nobutsuna. Nobutsuna's swordsmanship was compiled into one volume to preserve his knowledge by transmitting it to the student who strove to reach the highest level.

Having received the equivalent *menkyo kaiden* from the Taisha-ryu, Togo Shigekata became highly regarded within the Satsuma domain. He was expected to become the next master, but tragedy was to strike the Shimazu when they were forced to negotiate surrender to Hideyoshi in 1587. Despite having been totally overwhelmed by a massive army backed up by warships and firearms, the defeat was regarded by the Shimazu as a blow to their much-vaunted skills of swordsmanship. It had been a particularly bitter experience for *sensei* Higashi Shinnojo, who took it as a personal failure.

The following year the now-retired Satsuma daimyo Shimazu Yoshihisa (1533–1611) went to Kyoto to display his new loyalty to Hideyoshi. Togo Shigekata was ordered to go with him as his attendant, and took the opportunity when in the capital to improve his knowledge of swordfighting along with pursuing his other great passions, lacquerwork and goldsmithing. Most importantly, Shigekata made the acquaintance of the Soto Zen priest Zenkitsu (1567–94), who was a swordmaster of the Jigen-ryu, which emphasized the need for Zen meditation as part of the package of skills for a swordsman. This added an entirely new dimension to Shigekata's appreciation of the art of swordfighting, and he flourished as a pupil under Zenkitsu. The enthusiastic Shigekata was soon eager to prove the worth of his newly acquired teaching and yearned to return to Satsuma and his old *sensei*. This finally came about in 1601, when Yoshihisa's nephew Iehisa (1576–1638) succeeded his father Shimazu Yoshihiro as daimyo and took up office in Kagoshima.

Three years of hard practice and study were to follow Shigekata's return to Kyushu. The most important element of his physical regime was his own unique version of *suburi*, the sword-practice technique akin to shadow-boxing. The Jigen-ryu version was known as *tategi-uchi*, and consisted of repeatedly striking a wooden sword against a vertical wooden post (*tategi*). It is still practised within the modern Jigen-ryu to this day. The post, usually of oak or chestnut wood, stands about 2m above the floor. The swordsman, armed with a crude version of a *bokuto*, assumes the school's characteristic fighting posture, *tonbo gamae* ('dragonfly stance') 5–6m from the post.

Following a long, loud exclamation of '*kiai*' ('energy') he pounces upon the post at an appropriate distance and begins to strike it repeatedly. The keynote of the Jigen-ryu was expressed in the phrase '*Asa ni sanzen, yu ni hassen*' ('Three thousand in the morning and 8,000 in the evening'), indicating the enormous number of repetitions of blows required. Striking a wooden post so many times was exhausting and painful. Togo Shigekata had apparently first honed the technique by practising on persimmon trees growing within the grounds of the Shimazu mansion, until none was left. The exclamation of *kiai* helped in the endeavour, and Togo Shigenori, the 12th-generation *sensei* of the Jigen-ryu, explained its purpose as follows:

Yamaguchi Jiro, one of the swordsmen of the Shinsengumi, is shown here in an ink painting housed at Goryokaku Fortress Museum in Hakodate, Hokkadio. He is trampling underfoot a samurai identified by his *mon* (badge) as a follower of the Shimazu of Satsuma – the deadliest enemies of the pro-shogun Shinsengumi.

In my school we perform a loud and sustained *kiai* with the shout of 'Ei!' It is only when we are breathing out that we pay attention to carefully using our strength. According to our tradition the employment of *kiai* dominates the opponent, enhances our strength and enables one to strike hard. In former times the use of *kiai* sometimes went too far, and practitioners damaged their throats, even spitting blood.

Understanding and practically applying the content of the written scrolls presented to him by the monk Zenkitsu confronted Shigekata with an equally daunting mental challenge. The effort led him into the study of esoteric Buddhism, particularly that of the Shingon sect, in which contemplative meditation on the utterance of a single syllable provided a religious parallel to the explosive *kiai*. This observation may be noted as an interesting example of a situation where the abstract notions of Zen Buddhism are realized through the rituals and practices of a different Buddhist sect.

The monk Zenkitsu, who instructed Togo Shigekata in swordfighting and its associated religious practices.

Even though the enthusiastic Togo Shigekata appeared to have brought with him from Kyoto a new and promising school of swordsmanship, the Taisha-ryu under Higashi Shinnojo was still the official school of the Satsuma clan. But as Togo Shigekata grew in his knowledge and application of the Jigen-ryu style, he became ever more convinced that after following the teachings of the Taisha-ryu the Shimazu had been defeated, so he perceived a need to replace this school. The Shimazu were traditionally very conservative, but the new daimyo, Iehisa, having spent much time in Kyoto, tended to favour the Jigen-ryu style above the Taisha-ryu. In 1604 he ordered a *taryu jiai* ('inter-school contest') between the two traditions. Shigekata was to fight for the Jigen-ryu while Higashi Shinnojo would represent the old Taisha-ryu, thus making the contest a deeply significant occasion for both parties. Shigekata's hard work bore fruit and he was victorious, so the Jigen-ryu then became the official school

A member of the modern Jigen-ryu in Kagoshima City practises *tategi-uchi* – the technique of striking a wooden pole repeatedly with a crude *bokuto*.

for the Shimazu daimyo. All Shigekata did then was to institute a very subtle change of name whereby the original Chinese characters reading *ji gen* ('self-discovery') were replaced by different characters representing the same sound but a different meaning, namely 'manifestation'. This derived from an expression in a Buddhist sutra on the manifestation on earth of miraculous divine power.

The subsequent close association of the Jigen-ryu with Satsuma has resulted in its becoming one of the most reliably documented swordfighting schools in Japan, and from its literature we may discover that the Jigen-ryu stressed three key points or principles, as follows:

'A sword should not be drawn from its scabbard unless it is to attack.'

This principle expressed the twin values of non-aggressive behaviour and Zen-like detachment from the world. The shogun Tokugawa Ieyasu once made a similar point when he commented that 'the right use of a sword is that it should subdue the barbarians while lying gleaming in its scabbard. If it leaves its sheath it cannot be said to be used rightly.' A Jigen-ryu anecdote used to illustrate this point concerns a swordsman who asked the master how he could win a swordfight, and received the answer that he would win if he did not draw his sword. This puzzled the pupil until one day he was suddenly attacked by an enemy and drew his sword almost unconsciously; when he came to his senses the enemy lay dead. The victory was ascribed to the fact that because of his training he was always 'geared up' and ready to fight, even without knowing it, but at the same time he would never actively seek to start a fight.

A modern martial arts practitioner in Hino, Tokyo, demonstrates the art of cutting into a rolled bamboo mat. This was a traditional practice routine for a swordsman, used against an object that would provide resistance to the blade similar to that given by human flesh.

'Do not doubt your first strike; the second strike never wins.'

This principle contrasts swordfighting in battle or combat with swordfighting in a sport such as *kendo*. In sport one can win point for point. In sword combat all that matters is the first point that is scored, which must be the death of one's enemy. This further stresses the emphasis implied by the first principle: that the deadly first strike should be enough and that all one's energy should be put into it with no mental deviation from it.

'The sword is the means of destroying your enemy, not a means of defence.'

This principle indicated how completely the Jigen-ryu had dispensed with the notion of the sword as a shield, whereby if the first blow was offered by one's opponent it could be countered and a deadly response offered. Instead the single, powerful and devastating first strike is all. This was the final realization of the power of the katana ready to leap from its scabbard.

'Never practise in public.'

The technique of Jigen-ryu was a secret one, about which the practitioner should be proud but never boastful. Public display reduces the art to travelling sideshow. Furthermore, practice alone makes the swordsman strong because he has to concentrate totally on what he is doing. There is no place for empty theatrical gestures.

To these principles, which set the Jigen-ryu somewhat apart from its contemporaries, may be added certain other features according to which it differed from other schools. First, the Jigen-ryu swordsman practised in everyday clothes in bare feet on a floor of hard beaten earth rather than on wooden flooring or *tatami* (straw mats). Second, the traditional act of bowing to one's opponent (the *rei*) was dispensed with, the only bow of respect given being one to the practice hall on entering and leaving. All these features may be seen today at the Jigen-ryu's *dojo* in Kagoshima City, where modern swordsmen practise with each other in the traditional way and also carry out a deafening *tategi-uchi*.

THE KATANA IN THE IKEDAYA INCIDENT, 1864

The political upheavals that convulsed Japan in the mid-nineteenth century resulted in more examples of katana use, sometimes on a large scale, than at any time since the Sengoku Period.

One of the most violent and best recorded is the Ikedaya Incident, when an inn located in a quiet corner of Kyoto unexpectedly became a scene of carnage. The contrast between this encounter and the fight between armoured men at the sieges of Minowa and Namweon is most interesting, and there are few better examples of the destructive power of a katana in the hands of a skilled swordsman than this detailed account that has come down to us from the year 1864.

This attack on the Ikedaya was carried out by members of the shogun's special police corps, the *Shinsengumi*, whose role it was to protect Kyoto against the terror attacks of the anti-Tokugawa factions. Their victims were imperial loyalists from the Choshu fief in western Japan, who had gathered in the capital to plan an audacious coup involving the virtual kidnapping of the emperor. The fight at the Ikedaya pitted swordsman against swordsman and sword against sword, with little in the way of armour or other protection for either man or blade, and eyewitness accounts also testify to the enormous destruction wrought upon inferior katana blades by superior swords. The human cost in lives and wounds was of course more tragic and more terrible in this brief conflict, which became one of the last sword-against-sword clashes of pre-modern Japan.

The background to the fight at the Ikedaya lies in the political tensions that arose following the arrival of Western ships in Japanese waters a decade earlier. This situation took Japan almost to the brink of civil war. Two factions had developed: those who believed Japan should open its doors to the foreigners and those who maintained that this intrusion into the 'land of the gods' should be resisted at all costs. The former position was that taken by the Tokugawa shogun, and one of the shogun's chief

This wooden statue is of Kondo Isami, leader of the Shinsengumi during the Ikedaya Incident of 1864. He is shown holding his sword, 'Kotetsu', in his hand. This fine blade took a great deal of punishment during the raid on the Ikedaya.

advisors, Ii Naosuke, had been murdered because of it. Opposition to the Tokugawa took the form of demanding the expulsion of the foreigners and, if necessary, the abolition of the shogunate itself and its replacement by a new government ruling in the name of the emperor. Following these principles, the reactionary forces became imperial loyalists – a status that was to aid them greatly when the inevitable civil war began in 1868. However, in 1864 both sides were little more than rival factions who used their katana for murder and terror.

So dangerous had the situation become in Kyoto, where the emperor resided, that the shogun had appointed a loyal kinsman called Matsudaira Katamori, daimyo of Aizu, as Protector of Kyoto. To help him protect the imperial capital against loyalist violence, Katamori recruited his own corps of skilled swordsmen. These men were not hereditary retainers of the Tokugawa but instead just *ronin* ('men of the waves' – unemployed warriors), some not from the samurai class. Changing the last character in their title, Matsudaira Katamori called them instead '*roshi*' ('samurai of the waves'), a name he felt was more suited to their egalitarian nature and to the superb swordfighting skills, the sole criteria by which they had been selected. However, the majority of the *roshi* proved to be politically unsuitable and fell prey to loyalist propaganda. Nevertheless, 13 of their number pledged true loyalty to the shogun and to the Protector of Kyoto, and were then 'newly selected' by him – hence the name 'newly selected corps', or *Shinsengumi*.

One of the Shinsengumi's leaders, and a man who was to play a central role in the Ikedaya Incident, was Kondo Isami (1834–68), who was born of farming stock in Musashi province. Despite his non-samurai background Kondo had joined a *kenjutsu* school in Edo and trained until he became an expert swordsman. He was as committed to perfection in swordfighting as anyone born within the social class to which he aspired, and into which he had effectively been thrust. His determination to succeed was shown by the robe he wore when training, which bore a white death's head on the back. Kondo's closest friend was Hijikata Toshizo, who would become a deputy commander of the Shinsengumi. A year younger than Kondo, he came from a similar social background.

The Shinsengumi were based in the vicinity of the Mibudera Temple, an area now swallowed up by modern metropolitan Kyoto. From there the Shinsengumi members patrolled the streets of the capital. They were instantly recognizable by the garish uniform they chose for themselves: a light blue *haori* (jacket) with pointed white designs on the sleeves.

The Igagoe vendetta prompted one of the most celebrated mass swordfights in Edo Period Japan. This combat involved a revenge attack at the crossroads near the castle town of Iga-Ueno.

They wore headbands and carried a flag on which was inscribed the ideogram for *makoto* ('sincerity'). Their appearance was equalled in drama by the severe code of conduct they drew up for themselves, violation of which was punishable by ritual suicide. Needless to say, many hours were given to the practice of swordfighting, including methods that went far beyond any seen in a martial arts *dojo*. In order to prepare the members for the rigours of street fighting and the ever-present dangers of a surprise attack, sleeping Shinsengumi members could be woken by a comrade wielding a real sword and ordered to defend themselves. Every day the Shinsengumi would go out on patrol, and often crossed swords with imperial loyalists. They bragged to each other about how successful they had been. One claimed that the blood of a man he had killed splattered on the ridge of the adjacent house, another that the blood of the man he had cut down had reached the roof.

While the Shinsengumi were carrying out their savage armed patrols on the streets of Kyoto, their rivals were plotting revolution. The Ikedaya Incident came about as a result of rumours that one of the most fanatical of the loyalist fiefs, Choshu, was planning to take matters into its own hands and mount a coup against the emperor. Rumours that Choshu was planning to attack the imperial palace had been rife for some time, and events were to show that these fears were well founded. The essence of the Choshu plot was that the insurgents should take over the palace in a raid. This would no doubt attract the attention of the Protector of Kyoto and his Shinsengumi, who would be summarily dealt with. The emperor would then be taken to distant Choshu, where he would be forced to issue a decree abolishing the shogunate and ordering the expulsion of the foreigners.

A life-sized diorama at Sakamoto Ryoma Memorial Museum in Nochi on Shikoku Island depicts a member of the Shinsengumi in traditional costume. The incident depicted is the murder of Ryoma.

Interrogating and torturing Choshu suspects enabled the Shinsengumi to piece together the details of the plot. They also learned that Choshu loyalists frequented an inn called the Ikedaya. They already knew that a shopowner who lived nearby, Furudaya Shuntaro, had sheltered loyalists and a raid on his shop revealed a cache of weapons. Shuntaro was taken back to Mibudera and hung upside down from a rope in a storehouse. After half an hour of torture he revealed every detail of the plot. On hearing of Shuntaro's arrest the more sensible of the Choshu plotters advocated abandoning their scheme and hastily returning to western Japan. Others called for a quick raid on the Shinsengumi headquarters to rescue Shuntaro, if he was still alive, and then carrying out the coup as originally planned. They resolved to meet that night at the Ikedaya to make a final decision. It was to prove a fateful error of hesitation.

That same evening the Shinsengumi went out to track down the plotters, their modest complement of 34 men having been augmented by other pro-Tokugawa samurai based in Kyoto. Two main groups set off on either side of the Kamo River. Hijikata Toshizo followed the eastern bank, Kondo Isami the western. Expecting armed resistance, the Shinsengumi members had chosen to wear light armour under their robes. The protection was modest – only a 7kg chainmail shirt and gloves for the body – but some also wore a light iron helmet with a mail hood for their heads and necks. The loyalists, who were not prepared for any intervention, had no protection at all. The Ikedaya was to be the main focus of the Shinsengumi's attentions, but the two sides could hardly have chosen a less sinister night for what was about to happen. The citizens of Kyoto were making ready for the annual Gion Festival, one of the greatest shrine celebrations in Japan. The streets were thronged with happy crowds enjoying the celebrations beneath paper lanterns in the warm summer air.

Kondo's unit arrived at the Ikedaya at about ten o'clock that night and quickly realized that their quarry was inside. Astonishingly, it seems the Choshu plotters mounted no guard. Instead they were upstairs getting drunk. The noise they were making betrayed their presence to the Shinsengumi, ten of whom stepped over the threshold into the small inner courtyard. Four – Kondo, Nagakura, Okita and Todo – entered the inn itself, where they found a stack of weapons. The six who stayed outside on guard quickly tied the weapons together in a bundle so that they could not be used. Yet still the plotters were oblivious of their presence, and Kondo Isami even had to announce their arrival by summoning the proprietor. The man panicked and ran upstairs with the four Shinsengumi behind him. On the upper floor the raiders encountered about 20 of the plotters, one of whom attacked the Shinsengumi with his sword and was cut down with one stroke. Several made a rush for the stairs and the illusion of safety below. Kondo followed them.

Downstairs, one of the Shinsengumi suddenly started coughing up blood – not from a sword wound but from tuberculosis, which would one day kill him. He retired from the scene while the others took up guard positions outside the Ikedaya, expecting the rest of the plotters to break out of the inn. Kondo Isami took up his own position at the rear of the inn. Nagakura stood near the front entrance while Todo stood guard over the courtyard garden. Reinforcements under Hijikata Toshizo soon arrived, just as one of the Choshu men appeared from the front door. Tani Sanjuro, who had just arrived with Hijikata, stabbed him with a spear and Nagakura finished him off with a swordstroke. A second man appeared and received a slashing stroke from Nagakura's sword that sliced open his upper body below the shoulder. One man who had run down the stairs earlier was discovered hiding in the privy in the courtyard and was killed without mercy.

The desperate Choshu samurai now realized that they were cornered. Other pro-Tokugawa samurai had now arrived, so those left within the Ikedaya decided to make a spirited charge at their besiegers with their swords drawn. Nagakura later recalled that the Choshu samurai came at them like cornered rats, swinging their swords so fiercely against the Shinsengumi that Togo's light helmet was knocked clean off his head from a blow. The cut on his forehead made blood run into his eyes, temporarily blinding him. The same man then attacked Nagakura, the tip of his sword ripping into his shirt just before the skin. Using his katana Nagakura blocked a further slash towards his wrist and delivered a counter-stroke that hit the man on the side of his face, cutting his throat to the neck. Blood spurted over them both as he fell. It was only then that Nagakura realized that his hand had received a deep cut.

The Shinsengumi leader Kondo Isami was fully involved in the fighting, taking on four or five men and narrowly avoiding being wounded himself. His skills as a swordfighter were dramatically demonstrated, but Kondo was later to attribute his success and survival largely to the quality of his katana. He wrote about his sword as follows:

We fought against a large number of rebels. The sparks flew. After we had fought for a couple of hours Nagakura's sword had been broken in two, Okita's sword had been broken off at the tip, the blade of Todo's sword had been cut up like a bamboo whisk ... my sword, perhaps because it is the prize sword *Kotetsu*, was unscathed ... Although I have been in frequent battles ... our opponents were many and all courageous fighters, so that I nearly lost my life.

The reference 'the prize sword *Kotetsu*' is to a blade that Isami had purchased before going to Kyoto. As a result of his training he regarded himself as a fine swordsman and desired a blade to match, and so he acquired a fine sword by Nagasone Kotetsu (1605–78), a celebrated early Edo Period master of the Shinto era. The sword certainly seems to have been worth having, although rumours circulated that the famous blade was actually a forgery made by an unscrupulous living swordsmith who inscribed Kotetsu's signature on the tang and sold it through a third party to the unwitting Kondo Isami. Other experts claimed that the sword was genuine. Whatever its provenance, it was strong and resilient enough to withstand one of the fiercest tests ever applied to a blade outside the battlefield situation. Other blades broke, and there is a later eyewitness account of the Shinsengumi marching away from the Ikedaya waving swords with bent blades, but Kondo Isami's prize katana saved his life.

Three of the newly arrived Shinsengumi then entered the house and four of their opponents allowed themselves to be captured. More Shinsengumi arrived and dashed upstairs. Very soon a wounded conspirator fell through the ceiling and was despatched in the room below.

A later assessment of the Ikedaya Incident counted seven Choshu supporters killed outright, with a further four dying later from their wounds. Twenty-three of them were captured. Other samurai present with them were hunted down, some of them committing suicide in the streets around about to avoid the disgrace of capture. One, Mochiyuki Kameyata from the fief of Tosa, escaped only to be apprehended later by a group of Aizu samurai. He cut the left arm off one and split open the face of another. Badly wounded himself, he managed to flee towards the Choshu estate in Kyoto, but feeling his strength diminishing he committed *hara-kiri* with his *wakizashi* rather than be captured alive. Elated by their victory, the Shinsengumi marched back to the Mibudera watched by crowds of onlookers, who gasped when the victorious samurai brandished their broken and damaged swords. The horrific scene they had left behind at the Ikedaya was later described by Nagakura Shinpachi as follows:

> Not one of the paper screen doors was left intact, all of them having been smashed to pieces. The wooden boards of the ceiling were also torn apart when men who had been hiding under the floorboards were stabbed with spears from below. The *tatami* mats in a number of

Ikedaya, 1864 (previous pages)

The Ikedaya Incident of 1864 was one of the most savage swordfights to occur around the time of the Meiji Restoration. The shogun's police corps, the Shinsengumi, cornered a group of imperialist revolutionaries from Choshu in the Ikedaya Inn and cut them to pieces. The illustration depicts the height of the raid, when the Shinsengumi in their blue jackets overcame the feeble resistance put up by the unprepared plotters.

rooms, both upstairs and downstairs, were spotted with fresh blood. Particularly pitiful were arms and feet, and pieces of facial skin with the hair still attached scattered about.

Thus ended one of the last and most ghastly demonstrations of the power of the katana in the whole of Japanese history. Yet four years later the shogun that the Shinsengumi had fought to protect was forced to resign, and in the turbulence that followed Kondo Isami was ambushed and shot with a bullet through his shoulder. It was a bad wound, but fortunately kept him away from the catastrophic defeat of the Tokugawa army at the battle of Toba-Fushimi in January 1868. In Kondo's place his longstanding comrade Hijikata Toshizo led the Shinsengumi against the artillery fire of the Satsuma imperial forces. It was the first time these expert swordsmen had been subjected to cannon fire, and they responded with a brave but futile charge with drawn swords during which 30 Shinsengumi members were killed. The survivors were evacuated via Osaka, where they picked up their convalescing commander Kondo Isami and travelled by ship to Edo. Their fighting spirit was remarkably undiminished, although Hijikata Toshizo was forced to acknowledge: 'Swords and spears will no longer be of use in battle. They are simply no match for guns.' But with a pragmatism that echoed the adoption of modern weapons by their enemies, he ordered a consignment of state-of-the-art breechloading rifles for Japan's most famous swordfighters. Nevertheless he eventually went to his own death on a horse with a drawn katana in his hand.

IMPACT
The Japanese icon

THE SWORD IN THE AGE OF THE GODS

As noted earlier, swords have been present throughout Japanese history as a weapon, but the impact of the sword both culturally and militarily has evolved over the centuries. It has shifted from being a secondary although highly regarded weapon to a vivid symbol that has become an extension of the samurai himself, influencing Japanese art and literature.

In terms of its impact on Japanese culture, the sword has played a vital role from ancient times as a potent symbol of power and the authority to rule. The Isonokami sword, gift of the King of Baekje, represents a historical reality to which various legendary and mythological interpretations have been attached, but there is one other ancient weapon to be considered. This is the earliest cultural image of the sword, and appears in Japanese imperial mythology under the name *Kusanagi* – the 'Grass-Mowing Sword'. Kusanagi acts as a direct spiritual link between the world of men and the world of Japan's ancestral *kami* through its inclusion as one of the three sacred objects of the Japanese emperors – their 'crown jewels'. No other sword in Japanese history has become so powerful a symbol.

The appearance of the sword Kusanagi takes us right back to one of the most important of all the Japanese creation myths: the story of the tempestuous relationship between Amaterasu, Goddess of the Sun, and her younger brother Susa-no-o. The well-known tale tells of Susa-no-o's outrageous behaviour, which included breaking down the barriers between the rice fields and letting horses loose in the fields. We may regard these as symbolic behaviours that were injurious to fertility and agriculture, and in a shocking challenge to the ritual purity of his sister, Susa-no-o first defecates inside Amaterasu's palace, then drops the body of a flayed colt through the roof so as to alarm her. Frightened by this, Amaterasu hides in a cave, thus denying light to the world. She stays there until she is enticed out, to great rejoicing.

The myth continues with an account of Susa-no-o's journey to Izumo province (modern Shimane Prefecture), a part of Japan that is second only to Yamato in the amount of detail included in the creation stories. Historians and archaeologists generally believe this is because the court that held sway in Izumo was a major rival to Yamato, and the Susa-no-o stories support this because they depict in mythological form the surrender of influence by Izumo to Yamato. Yet within this relationship we encounter a subtle transformation of Susa-no-o's image from simply that of a wild younger brother to a great bearer of culture who brings the skills of metalworking across the seas from Korea. Settling in Izumo, Susa-no-o uses his sword, the product of the technological innovation he brought, to provide a great service to the local people by killing a fierce eight-headed dragon. He first gets the dragon drunk on *sake* (each head has to drink) and then slays it as it sleeps:

> Then Susa-no-o drew the ten-span sword which he wore and chopped the serpent into small pieces. When he came to the tail, the edge of his sword was slightly notched, and he therefore split open the tail and examined it. In the inside there was a sword. This is the sword which is called *Kusanagi no tsurugi* … its original name was *Ama no murakumo* ('Cloud Cluster'). Susa-no-o said: 'This is a divine sword. How can I presume to appropriate it to myself?' So he gave it up to the gods of heaven.

We see encapsulated in this myth Susa-no-o as the introducer of metalworking and his submission to the Yamato, symbolized by his handing over the magical sword to his sister. Amaterasu later gives the sacred sword, together with the mirror and the jewel comprising the other two sacred emblems, to her grandson Ninigi when he takes possession of the Earth. Ninigi eventually passes the three items on to his grandson Jimmu, identified as the first emperor of Japan, to whom are given the traditional dates of 660–585 BC. The three items were then handed down as the symbols of sovereignty from one emperor to the next, with only the sword Cloud Cluster being put to warlike use. This incident occurred during the life of Prince Yamato. Yamato was the son of Emperor Keiko, the 12th emperor according to the traditional reckoning, who sent Prince Yamato off on a military campaign. Before leaving for war Prince Yamato

In this image, part of a hanging scroll from Ikitsuki Local History Museum, Nagasaki Prefecture, dated 1832, Matsuura Kankansai, the daimyo of Hirado, is shown seated with his *wakizashi* in his belt. His very ornate *tachi* appears in a swordstand at his side.

67

called in at the Great Shrine of Ise where his aunt was high priestess. To arm him for his campaign she gave him the Cloud Cluster sword, and Yamato put it to good use when he was ambushed in the province of Sagami. After Prince Yamato had been fooled into entering a grassy plain, his enemies set fire to the grass to burn him to death, but Yamato cut through the burning grass and made a path to safety. Thus it was that the sacred sword acquired its familiar name (in full) *Kusanagi no tsurugi* ('Grass-Mowing Sword').

SWORD PRACTICE AND TRAINING

The supreme manifestation of the artistry of the katana was of course found in its use for fighting rather than as a religious symbol. Here, the *kengo* managed to combine the practical artistry of the katana with deep philosophical meanings. However, they were always faced with one great dilemma: how could the sword's greatest qualities be realized without bringing about someone's death? Even in a friendly contest with real swords the slightest mistake on behalf of one combatant could have led to

This remarkable statuette shows two swordsmen wearing the protective armour introduced for sword practice during the eighteenth century. The armour closely resembles modern *kendo* gear.

a death. One solution was *suburi* – a drilling method whereby the sword was swung over and over against an imaginary opponent; this technique was taken to its extreme by the Jigen-ryu of Satsuma, as described above. A student could also perform *kata* – employing a standard practice method found in Japanese martial arts today, which involves performing set moves or forms in a precise and prescribed manner.

The most realistic experience achievable without using sharp edges was by using *bokuto* – the wooden swords made in the general shape of a real sword and with a real sword's approximate weight. To compensate for the higher density of steel in a real sword the blade was made about an inch thick. Since samurai practising with *bokuto* would not wear protective armour, but fought instead with unmasked faces and unprotected sleeves, savage blows could still be sustained. This could lead to severe bruising and the occasional broken limb, and it is a measure of the degree to which the *bokuto* was able to provide an authentic substitute for a katana that they were often chosen for serious competitive duels between rivals who wished to establish their superiority without causing death.

Sometimes *bokuto* fighters would 'pull their punches' before the opponent was actually struck and achieve a victory 'on points'. This technique, also used in real-sword practice sessions, was called *tsumeru*. To be praised for one's *tsumeru*, especially in the heat of a contest, was one of the greatest compliments a swordsman could receive. However, this was always difficult to achieve, and it was equally difficult to judge whether a victory had been gained in the split second in which the decisive blow was laid. *Tsumeru* was a speciality of the famous Miyamoto Musashi. According to one of the many stories told about him, he could so perfectly control the blow from his katana that he could sever a grain of rice placed on a man's forehead without drawing blood.

The only way a samurai could legally practise his swordsmanship skills against living bodies was by executing criminals. In *Hagakure*, Yamamoto Tsunetomo records: 'Last year I went to the Kase execution grounds to try my hand at beheading, and I found it to be an extremely good feeling.' Formerly, he tells us, all the young samurai were expected to have carried out a beheading by the age of about 15, and even five-year-olds could use swords to kill dogs. A more merciful alternative was to hack at bundles of bamboo or straw *tatami* mats.

Towards the end of the sixteenth century a new practice weapon, the *shinai*, was introduced by Kamiizumi Nobutsuna. The original *shinai*, almost identical to the weapon used in modern *kendo*, consisted of a number of light bamboo blades tied together. If some form of protective armour was worn blows could be delivered using all the power in a samurai's forearms, and enabled what one might term 'full-contact *kenjutsu*' to be practised. From the early eighteenth century onwards samurai used protection for the face and forearms similar to modern *kendo* armour, but *shinai* and armour were always abandoned for serious contests and *bokuto* used instead. Through furious *bokuto* contests and in the much rarer instances of fighting to the death using real swords, *kengo* lifted the art of the katana to its ultimate height.

THE SWORD AND ART

The swordsman as artist is best exemplified by the strange figure of Miyamoto Musashi, whose story has been so obscured by legend that it is difficult to disentangle the man from the myth. He comes over as a peculiar character, solitary and obsessive, whose skills with the sword are unquestioned and greatly admired, but which at the same time make him feared and disliked. His life consisted of a series of wanderings, short periods in the service of various daimyo, numerous duels, and an increasingly deep philosophical insight into swordsmanship, taking its final form in the famous *Gorinsho* ('Book of Five Rings') which he completed shortly before his death in 1645. Miyamoto Musashi made an outstanding contribution to the literature surrounding swordfighting. He was also a skilled painter, and ink paintings by him are much admired as examples of Zen-inspired art.

Miyamoto Musashi also respected the sword for its own artistic merits, a trait he held in common with most of his contemporaries. The connoisseurship that clearly existed among the daimyo and samurai of the Sengoku Period is shown by their appreciation of a sword for its intrinsic beauty as much as its fighting quality. One particular anecdote about Toyotomi Hideyoshi tells us about personal preferences regarding swords:

The young swordsman Sasaki Ganryu was Miyamoto Musashi's most celebrated opponent. This statue of him stands at the head of the valley of Ichijodani in Fukui Prefecture – the site of one of their encounters. He is holding a *bokuto* (wooden practice sword).

At one time when Hideyoshi saw five swords left in the main hall of Fushimi Castle, he said to his men: 'Just for fun, I will guess who are the owners of these swords,' and began to point from one sword to another, and guessed correctly. One of the impressed men praised him, saying: 'Truly, you are a genius, sir, blessed with god-like knowledge!' The laughing Hideyoshi replied: 'It is easy, since I know the personality of the owners. For example, this gold-inlaid sword must belong to Ukita Hideie since he loves something extravagant. This long one must belong to Uesugi Kagekatsu, whose father preferred a longer sword. Maeda Toshiie, who is now lord of a large province thanks to his military merit, still loves his old sword with a haft bound in leather. So this sword belongs to no one other than Toshiie. This one with a strange decoration must belong to Môri Terumoto, who favours something exotic. That one with nothing special must belong to Tokugawa Ieyasu, who is strong and great enough to discount his sword. He does not need to attract attention to his sword, and prefers an ordinary one with no special designs and decorations. Thus I have guessed, and my assumptions are correct.'

A connoisseur appreciates the quality of his finest blade, resting his sword hand on his left hand so that the detailing on the sword may be picked up in the available light.

These two qualities of fighting strength and artistic merit were major considerations when swords were given as gifts. So we read that after the battle of Nagashino in 1575 Okudaira Sadamasa, who had defended Nagashino Castle so valiantly against the besiegers led by Takeda Katsuyori, was presented by Tokugawa Ieyasu with a fine sword made by Yoshimitsu, which Ieyasu had himself received from Oda Nobunaga on account of his own exploits at the battle of Anegawa in 1570. A few years later Tomura Yoshikuni, a retainer of Satake Yoshinobu, displayed courageous conduct at the battle of Imafuku (1614), during which he was knocked unconscious. He was summoned to Nijo Castle in Kyoto and from the shogun Tokugawa Hidetada received an official letter of commendation and a fine sword. His comrade-in-arms Umezu Noritada, the 'Yellow Devil of the Satake Clan', also received a sword in recognition of his exploits at Imafuku.

To present a sword to one's valiant comrades was an occasion of great honour, but to allow a defeated enemy to retain his own sword was the supreme expression of both trust and self-confidence. This is shown by the interviews Toyotomi Hideyoshi held with Shimazu Yoshihisa and the Shimazu's veteran retainer Niiro Musashi-no-kami Tadamoto following the defeat of the Shimazu in the Kyushu campaign of 1587:

> 'You have opposed our emperor for the past 15 years, and should be punished as an imperial traitor. However, since you have come to greet me like this, you should be spared. Hereafter, we should communicate well with each other. I see you are without a sword, which is commendable for the occasion. Now, take this.' Hideyoshi took out one of his own swords, held the end of the sheath, and offered it to Yoshihisa. Hearing this, more people were impressed by Hideyoshi's valour and largesse.
>
> When Hideyoshi had an interview with Niiro Tadamoto, a subject of Yoshihisa, he ... took out a long sword named 'Cricket-Head', held it by its end, and offered it to him. The awestruck Tadamoto received it and took it home where he said to his young men, 'Hideyoshi is not a man for me to fight. He impressed me so much today.' Tadamoto had thought of stabbing Hideyoshi at the interview.

Such was the awesome power of the katana in the right hands: it could defeat an enemy simply by being handed to him.

CONCLUSION

THE KATANA: REVOLUTION OR EVOLUTION?

When undertaking an overview of the place of the katana in samurai history it is tempting to conclude that the weapon revolutionized Japanese warfare. However, this is to mistake evolution for revolution. The changes wrought in the manufacture and use of the sword in Japan were so subtle and took place over such a long period that it is almost impossible to identify any changes in the practice of warfare than can be directly attributed to the sword itself, apart from the introduction of the curved blade. Even the significance of the latter factor is hard to assess due to confusion about the date and circumstances of the curved-blade innovation. Instead, to some extent, the katana *is* samurai warfare. The weapon is always present at the samurai's side, and it is impossible to understand the samurai without appreciating the role of the sword as a weapon, a symbol and an extension of the man himself. These points were dramatically illustrated by the horrified reaction among the samurai class to the abolition of sword-wearing by the Meiji government. The likely reaction to any such ban was anticipated as early as 1871 by the English diplomat Lord Redesdale, who wrote in his classic *Tales of Old Japan*:

> The statesman who shall enact a law forbidding the carrying of this deadly weapon will indeed have deserved well of his country; but it will be a difficult task to undertake, and a dangerous one. I would not give much for that man's life. The hand of every swashbuckler in the country would be against him.

As it turned out, the ban on sword-wearing was to be but one element in the lead up to the total abolition of the samurai class; this itself formed a major plank of the modernizing reforms aimed at creating the 'New Japan'. The fine details of the reforms included symbolic gestures such as the banning of

73

Sakamoto Ryoma (1836–1867), one of the heroes of the Meiji Restoration, was a samurai who embraced modernity. The duality of this is neatly captured in this photograph: he is dressed as a perfect two-sword samurai, but with the addition of American-made leather boots!

the samurai's pigtail, but the ban on wearing swords by all but members of the armed forces was one of the main causes of protest from conservative samurai. Such an act was doubly insulting to the samurai class because it reduced the role of the katana, the greatest symbol of their aristocracy and authority, to being no more than just one weapon used by the new imperial army. This army was being created by conscription from among all social classes, not just the hereditary warrior class. Lord Redesdale's predictions were indeed borne out in a petition presented by a Kyushu samurai to the government. This individual saw the wearing of swords as a civil right and a valuable safeguard of law and order. The novelist Yukio Mishima quotes from the statement in his *Homba* ('Runaway Horses'). The reference to ancient times provides an interesting link with the early swords and swordbearers of Japan:

In my view the bearing of swords is a custom that characterized our land even in the ancient era of the gods and Emperor Jimmu. It is closely bound up with the origins of our country, it enhances the dignity of the imperial throne, solemnises the rites of our gods, banishes the spirits of evil, and puts down disorders. The sword, therefore, not only maintains the tranquillity of the nation but also guards the safety of the individual citizen. Indeed, the one thing essential to this martial nation that reveres the gods, the one thing that can never be set aside even for one moment, is the sword. How then, could those upon whom is laid the burden of fashioning and executing a national policy that honours the gods and strengthens our land be so forgetful of the sword?

This type of reaction to the Meiji government's diktats received its final expression through Saigo Takamori's Seinan War of 1877 – the conflict better known in the West as the Satsuma Rebellion. Saigo Takamori had been one of the great heroes of the Restoration Wars. It was his opposition to the policies of the Meiji emperor whose throne he had secured that made this elder statesman, who was treated by contemporaries with a degree of adulation comparable to that of the Duke of Wellington after Waterloo, lead an insurrection that was both reactionary and futile. From the start the Satsuma Rebellion was seen in a romantic light by contemporary commentators who ignored the fact that Saigo was at the forefront of modern military technology. One European correspondent wrote:

Saigo's men were but partly armed with rifles. Most of them were equipped with the keen double-handed swords of feudal times and with daggers and spears. It seemed to be their opinion that patrician samurai could rush into close quarters with the *heimin* (common people) and easily rout them – granting even that they were armed with rifles and bayonets. And it was reported that the astute Saigo ordered his soldiers not to kill the poor plebs in the government ranks, but rather to slash them well about the legs so as to disable them and render it necessary for each man thus wounded to be borne off the field by two able-bodied comrades – thus depriving the opposing ranks of three soldiers instead of one.

All this is undoubtedly a romantic exaggeration. Saigo Takamori was not such an extreme conservative as to believe that samurai swords and bravery were all an army needed at this time. The sword was indeed the universal weapon, but in addition his soldiers carried Snider and Enfield rifles, some carbines and pistols, and enough ammunition to provide about 100 rounds per man. Nevertheless, as with the samurai of old their katana were at their sides, and during the most important operation of the Satsuma Rebellion – the attempt by Saigo to capture Kumamoto Castle – swords were drawn and used. Furious attacks were carried out on the castle ramparts. The Satsuma samurai, their ancestral swords in hand, clambered up the walls like suicide squads, only to be shot down by rifle fire from the conscript army. Many hand-to-hand combats took place on the black walls of Kumamoto as fanaticism met determination, with the old loyalty to the samurai way pitted against a new version of honour that united Japan in a classless devotion to the emperor.

Yokogawa Munetoshi was one of the 'Forty-Seven Ronin of Ako', and is seen here in his stage persona in *Chushingura* (the *kabuki* play based on the raid of 1703) of Yukukawa Munenori. Munetoshi was one of the raiders who used a katana as his primary weapon, and he is seen here wielding the sword as a lantern is thrown at him during the attack.

THE KATANA TODAY

When Japan began its policy of overseas expansion at the end of the nineteenth century the officers of its armed forces, many of whom were descended from samurai families, wore swords at their belts and would use them in hand-to-hand combat. The pathetic sight of hundreds of captured swords being piled up ready for destruction at the end of World War II is as powerful a visual image of the passing of a culture as the words written about the Satsuma Rebellion. Yet somehow the tradition of the sword and, thankfully, many actual swords survived the reaction, to take their place as objects redolent of history and as highly collectable works of art.

Today, there are museums of swords and places associated with master swordsmen dotted throughout Japan. The two great martial arts shrines of Katori and Kashima are accessible from Tokyo and Chiba. In Kashimajingu there is a statue of Tsukahara Bokuden, while the shrine itself stands impressively among giant trees. There is a small museum and Bokuden's grave lies a short taxi ride away. Yagyu village near Nara is an interesting and attractive place to visit, with many historical features including the Yagyu *dojo*. In Tokyo the Japanese Sword Museum is well regarded, although I have not yet visited it myself. Osafune in Okayama Prefecture is home to Osafune Sword Village, a complex that includes an excellent museum. Osafune is no theme park; as the major historical centre for Bizen swords, it constitutes a serious centre for the study of the Japanese sword. Demonstrations of swordmaking and sword-polishing and of working with fittings are held regularly, with visiting displays of fine swords being mounted in the museum. Osafune is also a centre where experts meet to assess swords. In Kumamoto City is the Shimada Museum of Arts, which has probably the best collection of memorabilia relating to Miyamoto Musashi.

One of the most accessible and welcoming of the traditional schools of swordsmanship is the Jigen-ryu of Kagoshima, where the 12th master of the school, Togo Shigenori – born in 1959 – founded the Jigen-ryu Shiryokan in 1997. The establishment includes a *dojo* where sword practice may be observed, bringing to life the historic traditions of the sword-wielding samurai.

GLOSSARY

bokuto	wooden practice sword
chokuto	ancient straight-bladed sword
daimyo	local lord
daisho	matching pair of katana and *wakizashi*
dojo	practice hall
do-maru	style of close-fitting armour (see also *haramaki*)
emishi	aboriginal inhabitants of northern Japan
gunkimono	war tale
ha	cutting edge of the sword
habuchi	visible white line along the length of a sword blade
hadagane	harder outer steel section of a sword
hamon	pattern of the *habuchi*
haramaki	style of close-fitting armour (see also *do-maru*)
'hitotsu no tachi'	'one stroke'; expression summarizing Bokuden's swordsmanship
horimono	carved decoration
ji	the surface of a blade
Jigen-ryu	'School of Self-Discovery'; school of swordfighting of Satsuma province
Kage-ryu	'Shadow School' of swordfighting
kajiya	blacksmith, also used for a swordsmith
kami	deity
kamidana	'god shelf' holding images of deities (*kami*)
kata	set forms for sword practice
katana	standard fighting sword
Katori Shinto-ryu	name of school of swordfighting
kengo	master swordsman
kenjutsu	swordfighting as a martial art
'kiai'	'energy'; exclamation at start of attack
kissaki	point of a blade
kofun	burial mound
Koto	'Old Swords' period (up to 1600)
kumade	bear-paw polearm
menkyo kaiden	secrets of the art
mune	back of the sword
musha shugyo	warrior pilgrimage
muto	'no sword' technique of swordfighting
naginata	glaive (polearm with curved blade)
nie	coarse granular particles in a blade's surface
nioi	microscopic particles in a blade's surface
nodachi	extra-long sword
odachi	extra-long sword
ronin	'men of the waves' – unemployed warriors
ryu(ha)	school or tradition
same	skin of the giant ray used in sword grips

satetsu	iron-bearing sand
saya	scabbard
sensei	a greatly honoured teacher, a master
seoidachi	'shoulder-sword'; back-carried *tachi*
shinai	light bamboo practice sword
shingane	softer inner steel section of a sword
Shinkage-ryu	'New Shadow School' of swordfighting
shinogi	central ridge along a sword blade
Shinsengumi	'newly selected corps'; shogun's corps of skilled swordsmen
Shinto	'New Swords' period (after 1600)
Shinto-ryu	Bokuden school of swordfighting
shogun	military dictator of Japan
suburi	individual sword practice resembling shadow boxing
sun	an inch
sunobe	the rough sword before it is tempered
tachi	the classic samurai sword slung from a belt
Taisha-ryu	name of school of swordfighting
tama hagane	raw steel pieces produced by the smelting of iron sand
tanto	short sword or dagger
taryu jiai	inter-school contest
tategi	vertical wooden post used in *suburi*
tategi-uchi	practice involving repeatedly striking a post with a wooden sword
tosho	swordsmith
tsuba	swordguard
tsuka	sword handle
tsumeru	practice technique involving 'pulling punches'
wakizashi	modern term for a short sword
Yagyu Shinkage-ryu	name of school of swordfighting
yoroi	box-like armour of twelfth-century mounted warrior

SELECT BIBLIOGRAPHY AND FURTHER READING

Bottomley, Ian, *An Introduction to Japanese Swords* (Leeds, 2008)

Harris, Victor, *Swords of the Samurai* (London, 1990)

Irvine, Gregory, *The Japanese Sword: The Soul of the Samurai* (London, 2000)

Kapp, Leon, et al., *The Craft of the Japanese Sword* (Tokyo, 1987)

Kawachi, Kunihira and Masao Manabe, with Stephen Comee (translator), *The Art of the Japanese Sword as Taught by the Experts* (Tokyo, 2004)

McCullough, Helen Craig, *The Taiheiki: A Chronicle of Medieval Japan* (REF: New York, 1959)

Rogers, John M., 'Arts of war in times of peace: swordsmanship in *Honcho Bugei Shoden, Monumenta Nipponica 46,2 (1991)* pp. 174–202

Sato, Kanzan, *The Japanese Sword* (Kodansha: Tokyo, 1983)

Takeda, Y., 'Ichigeki Hitsu Satsu no Jigen-ryu Tanjo' in *Kengo to Otokodate (Raibaru Gekitotsu Nihon shi)*, Vol. 7 (Tokyo, 1979)

Turnbull, Stephen, *The Samurai Swordsman: Master of War* (London, 2008)

Yumoto, John, *The Samurai Sword: A Handbook* (Rutland VT, 1958)

INDEX